HOW TO GET
YOUR DOG TO DO
WHAT YOU WANT

HOW TO GET YOUR DOG TO DO WHAT YOU WANT

A Loving Approach to Unleashing Your Dog's Astonishing Potential

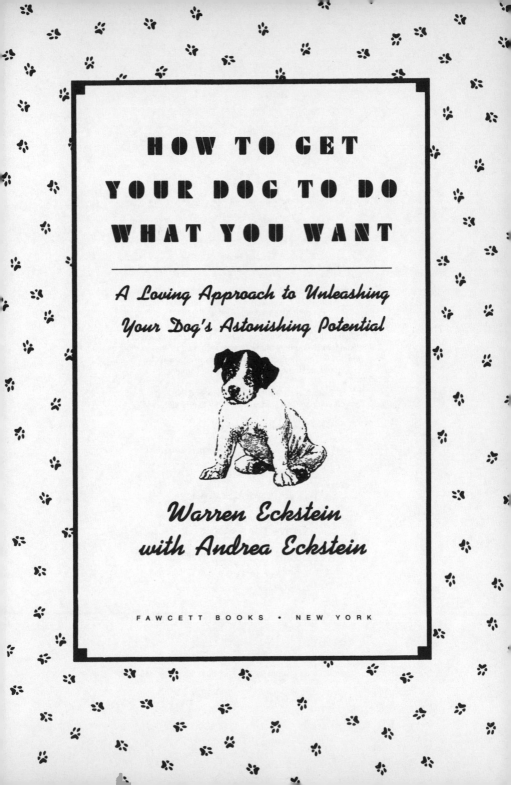

*Warren Eckstein
with Andrea Eckstein*

FAWCETT BOOKS · NEW YORK

A Fawcett Book
Published by The Random House Publishing Group

Copyright © 1994 by Warren Eckstein and Andrea Eckstein

Published in the United States by Fawcett Books, an imprint of
The Random House Publishing Group, a division of Random
House, Inc., New York,and simultaneously in Canada by
Random House of Canada Limited, Toronto.

Fawcett is a registered trademark and the
Fawcett colophon is a trademark of Random House, Inc.

www.ballantinebooks.com

Library of Congress Catalog Card Number: 94-94113

ISBN: 0-449-90956-5

Book design by JoAnne Metsch

Cover design by Judy Herbstman
Cover photo by Joe Levine

Manufactured in the United States of America

17 19 18

To my parents, Charles and Ruth Eckstein,
for all their love and devotion;
to my late wife Fay for all her support;
and in the memory of my friend and colleague Larry Hatzi

"In the beginning, God created man, but seeing him so feeble, He gave him the dog."

—Toussenel

I would like to thank my wife, Andrea,
for putting my thoughts down in words;
the thousands of animals who taught me so much;
and my four-footed "models"—
Jubare's Jazzmatazz, CH. Lumpos Betyar, CH.
Mar-Sher's Schaefer, CH. Tague's Scottish Legacy, CH.
Sandtree's Summer Legend, and the
Humane Society of New York's Paddy.

CONTENTS

CONTENTS

WHAT TO EXPECT FROM FIDO WHEN YOU'RE
  EXPECTING 80

SEX AND THE SINGLE DOG 85

CANINE KINDERGARTEN 94

CONTENTS

INTRODUCTION

Decades ago, owning a dog usually meant that Fido lived in a doghouse out on the family's property. Fido was rarely permitted in the house; instead, the backyard and the front porch were his domain. Of course, he was a loyal companion to his owners and a friendly playmate to his owners' children. More often than not, the family dog was named King, Princess, Duke, Dutchess, Fido, or Rover.

Today, it is not uncommon for the family dog to be named Sam, Sarah, Chester, Tiffany, Bob, or Suzy. This humanization of the family dog's name reflects a major change in the way people view their canine companions. No longer merely animals, our pets are now beloved members of the family. In fact, today, more likely than not, these four-footed family members live inside the home and, in many cases, even sleep in the family bed!

Because we have taken animals—specifically, dogs—into our human environment, we can no longer treat them as animals and expect them to respond like humans. Instead, we must learn to integrate them into our lives and help them become a part of our human life-style. With a little understanding and patience, we can live happily with our dogs and they can live happily with us.

I firmly believe that your dog is a member of your family. If you keep that in mind, if you truly feel it, your dog will act like one. That's one of the basic premises of this book. It's the best way I know to get your dog to do what you want.

Okay. Once you accept the premise, we've got to decide exactly how to treat the new family member.

It's really fairly simple—and the rest of this book is devoted to telling you just this: If you treat your dog with love, if you treat your dog with respect, if you treat your dog as if he or she is an intelligent, thinking animal capable of making decisions, your dog will respond in positive, astonishing ways.

But first you've got to understand not only that a dog thinks, but how and why he or she thinks.

Then and only then will you be able to get your dog to do what you want.

And you know what? By the time you reach that point, your dog is going to want to do the same things you want him or her to do. Not 100 percent of the time, of course. Nobody's perfect. Besides, if you want something that obeys your every command every single time, you don't want a dog—you want a robot! So go get a copy of *Popular Mechanics* or *Science Digest*. But if your goal is to turn Fido into an intelligent and loving member of the family, read on.

HOW TO GET
YOUR DOG TO DO
WHAT YOU WANT

WHAT YOU PUT IN IS
WHAT YOU GET OUT

As far as I'm concerned, a dog is a product of what's put into him. Two factors determine the personality, intelligence, and overall disposition of our canine companions: breeding—whether the parents were genetically well-suited to produce strong, healthy offspring (in the case of the randomly bred stray "generic" dog, whether the odds were in his favor), so that he was born physically sound, without inbreeding faults or any other genetic disorders—and environment—what the owner does or does not do with that dog. In other words, *you* play a tremendous role in influencing your dog's personality, intelligence, and disposition!

A DOG'S SELF-IMAGE

Dogs, just like people, have a strange way of living up—or down—to the image you project for them. Give them high expectations concerning their own abilities, and they'll reach for the stars trying to achieve them and please you. Downgrade their abilities by constantly telling them how displeased you are with their behavior, and you'll rip apart their self-esteem, making it impossible for them to believe in you and, most of all, in themselves.

Fido needs a good self-image if he's to attain the goals you set for him. I'm obviously not talking about graduating summa cum laude from Harvard or becoming the CEO of a Fortune 500 company, but I am talking about Fido attaining certain goals of good behavior—being socially well adjusted and blending well into your family unit, while also maintaining his own identity and psychological well-being. We take this for granted when everything is right with Fido. It's the sort of thing you don't think about until it's not there.

It's easy to tamper with how Fido feels about himself. There are three common ways. The first is a sin of omission—it often takes place without you even realizing it.

RIPPING APART FIDO'S SELF-IMAGE— WHAT NOT TO DO #1

By doing nothing, by ignoring your pet, by not interacting with him on a regular basis, you can do great damage. It is simply not enough just to feed and walk your dog, then treat him like a piece of furniture the rest of the time.

Yes, I know you lead busy lives and your time may be very limited, but dogs have a real need to have their egos stroked, to be told they're good, to understand how much they're loved. They need image- and confidence-building as much as we do. And they need a certain amount of self-esteem in order to behave well. They need to develop inner strength if they are to try something new or to learn to trust in you.

RIPPING APART FIDO'S SELF-IMAGE—
WHAT NOT TO DO #2

Bad-mouthing Fido and spreading gossip about him is the second way you can rip apart Fido's self-esteem and destroy his self-confidence, thereby creating psychological problems where they never before existed. Dogs are very astute and can sense a lot of what's going on around them. Many are so clever that they can even tell when you're speaking of them in unflattering terms to other people. They'll hang their heads in shame and drop their tails between their legs while you discuss their mistakes with the neighbors. I've often said, if you can't say something nice about your dog, don't say anything at all. Believe me, they know! Some dogs get embarrassed. Watch their faces and you'll see exactly what they're picking up. They know what's going on!

I once had a client who did nothing but complain about his dog. "Darn dog hair all over the place, darn walks on the coldest mornings of the winter, darn hard-to-open cans of dog food, darn this, darn that, darn dog." It was a bad situation, to say the least. The client was stressed out, with a lot of problems— trouble on the job, trouble with his ex-wife, trouble paying child support. Although I could certainly sympathize with him, I've never felt compassionate toward people who take out their problems on their pets, even though too many owners do exactly that.

This dog was so used to being scolded and verbally abused that every time she saw her owner coming, her behavior, due to sheer fear, took a turn for the worse. Pepper didn't mean to knock over the Parsons table and everything on it as she scrambled out of the way, but she couldn't help trying to escape as fast as possible when she saw her owner. Then Pepper piddled on the living room rug out of sheer nervousness. Later that evening after waking from her nap, she also didn't mean to stay, frozen with fear, in her owner's favorite easy chair. Pepper knew he wanted to sit in it, but her frightened, sleepy brain couldn't figure out what to do except sit there and growl as he tried to swat her out of the chair. That's when I was called in.

You see, what happened was that these two had set up a Catch-22. My client's berating behavior triggered Pepper's incorrect conduct, and her poor responses caused my client to react in an even worse fashion. His growing dislike of Pepper was crystal clear to her, and the ongoing battle actually affected her psychological balance. This was compounded by the fact that both Pepper and her owner had recently experienced the emotional upheaval of the divorce. Pepper in particular missed her human Mom and brothers and sisters. She became increasingly skittish and unhappy. The more they went at it, the more out of control things became. Pepper became so accustomed to hearing "bad dog, stupid dog, darn dog!" that she believed it. Everything she did seemed wrong, so as a result she did nothing right. The owner kept yelling and Pepper became submissive, then defensive, then slowly aggressive as she could take no more.

Was Pepper a bad dog? No, but she was caught up in a bad situation. I am a firm believer that stress can be transmitted from one end of the leash to the other. Yes, Pepper's owner was stressed out, but the fact remained that no one was nurturing Pepper or helping her develop a good self-image. Was Pepper in fact a good dog, a pretty dog, a nice dog? Yes she was—but nobody bothered to tell her so.

RIPPING APART FIDO'S SELF-IMAGE—
WHAT NOT TO DO #3

The most common way of undermining Fido's self-esteem occurs when dog owners get flooded with advice from well-intentioned friends, neighbors, and relatives, telling them to correct the dog for everything he does wrong. So these owners scold, yell, hit, step on back paws, knee, force Fido onto his back in a submissive position, squirt water pistols in his face, put hot sauce on his tongue, or stick his nose in his mess.

Dwell on the negatives long and often enough and you will actually help your dog develop a negative behavioral pattern whereby he gets so much attention for doing something wrong and, by comparison, so little attention for doing something right that he figures he might as well act badly. At least then he gets *some* attention, even though it's negative. Kids, you may know, sometimes do exactly the same thing.

For many dogs, "no" is the first word they hear in the morning when they're demanding a feeding or a walk from owners who are stumbling to the coffee pot with half-open eyes. "No" is also the last word they hear at night when they try to curl up on the bed with their owners. A lot of dogs constantly hear the word "no" for a variety of indiscretions, and it's this barrage of "no, no, no!" that undermines their self-esteem.

It's easy to ruin a dog's confidence this way. Most undermining is a result of old-fashioned thinking that Fido should always be corrected. He hears "no" for jumping on the company, "no" for eating the sandwich his owners left out on the kitchen table, "no" for helping navigate the car, and "no" for acting as a furry alarm clock at three A.M. I've been in many homes where I've said the word "no" and the family dog came running. These dogs have heard "no" so often, they think No is their name!

Educating our canine comrades should be a pleasurable experience, not a horror story. Of course, dogs will sometimes do the wrong things, but that's how they learn—that's how we all learn. It's inevitable that they'll soil the best carpet in the house (they seem to have an uncanny way of knowing just which one is the most expensive). And Fido may conduct his own taste test on your Gucci shoes or wooden bannister. But they can only learn what you want them to do by experimenting. How many of us as kids learned that the stove was hot only after we touched it? When it burned our fingers, we wanted a little comfort from our moms, not to get smacked in the face for touching it—our pride and fingers hurt enough already. And so it is with a dog's pride when he sees he's upset the people that love him most.

Remember, no matter whether they are huge Saint Bernards or tiny dachshunds, dogs are sensitive, emotional creatures with confidence that can be eroded, and they're fully capable of being embarrassed by their behavior—and the behavior of their owners.

THE "NO" SYNDROME

It's time to forget about the old-style mentality of raising Fido. Right now I can hear a lot of you saying that this "no, no, no!" syndrome could never happen to you. You would never be that constantly corrective when your wonderful, adorable dog makes a mistake. Well, you might be right, but a lot of owners still undermine their dog's self-esteem and pride to a lesser degree. This type of erosion, when compounded over a period of years, can have drastic results.

Think about this for a moment. What would you do if your dog chewed the armrest of your brand new leather chair, stole the filet mignon off your kitchen counter just before your guests arrived, and had an accident on the Oriental rug?

Regarding the first situation, I bet you'd bring him over to the chair, show him what he did wrong, and give him a smack. Even if it's not a hard smack, I bet over 50 percent of everyone reading this would give the dog at least a little swat. In the second situation, I bet you'd bring him over to the counter area, tell him "no," and give him a little swat. If you discovered the filet mignon was missing right after you discovered the destroyed chair, I bet the swat would be harder than what you'd ordinarily care to admit to. And for number three, the accident on the Oriental rug, you would probably bring him over to the mess, ask "What did you do?," scold or hit him, and maybe even rub his nose in it. If the accident happened right after the discovery of the chewed chair and the missing mignon, I bet those swats would be harder still.

Now let's review the answers. I'll bet that without you realizing it, you're already a victim of the "no" syndrome of dog training and behavior. After all, patience has its boundaries and is not limitless. Well, it doesn't have to be this way. We can love our dogs into good behavior.

BUILDING FIDO'S SELF-CONFIDENCE—
"YES" IS THE WAY TO GO

The easiest way to create a confident canine that behaves well is to spend more time focusing on the things the dog does right than correcting those he does wrong. Sure Fido gets plenty of corrections when he does number two where he's not supposed to—but do you spend the same or, better yet, more time kissing, hugging, stroking, and loving him when he relieves himself in the right place or performs some other minor feat? I doubt it. Most people don't. At best there's a "good boy" and a pat on the head. But what happened to "Yeah! What a good fella!" followed by kisses, hugs, a belly scratch, a head rub, more kisses, extra hugs, and then, when you're done, repeating the whole process all over again?

Your neighbors might find your antics a bit strange, but why should that stop you? Your dog will be well behaved, while they're struggling along for months or years with homes reeking like bad pet shops and full of chewed furniture. You'll always have the last laugh. I've even had people tell me their kids got potty trained at the same time they were working with Fido because of all the praising and loving going on. Now that's a fringe benefit if ever I heard one!

You must present a clear picture for your dog of exactly what makes you happy. Dogs usually don't have an opportunity to see this as clearly as we think they do. We all know that pets are willing to please their owners—so when they don't, don't you think it might be that their owners just aren't getting their points across? We don't have to dominate our dogs with corrective techniques, we just have to go overboard on all the things our four-footed best friends do properly. Believe me, they do more good things than you probably realize, so we must take the time to constantly tell them how wonderful they are. We must love, kiss, hug, and touch them for every positive accomplishment. Dogs that feel good about themselves will behave better for you. If you build their confidence, they will respond in kind. They must have a good self-image. If they think they're a failure at life, then what's the sense of trying? Let them know how smart, intelligent, and well loved they are. They'll live up to your expectations.

And please don't reserve your positive thoughts and actions only for those times when Fido has done something right. It's okay to tell him how wonderful he is for no reason at all. Stroke his ego and help him build a positive self-image. Tell him what a good dog he is, even if he's done nothing at all. Praise him, tell him he's wonderful, and give him a hug and a kiss for no reason. And while you're at it, give him a hug and a kiss for me.

DOES FIDO THINK?

I hope someone from up above will help me, because I know I'm going to get myself in a lot of hot water with what I'm about to say. One of the most heated debates between myself and many clinically trained behaviorists and psychologists is over whether dogs have the ability to think and make decisions. Many people who study animal behavior maintain that most animals don't think or make independent decisions. Instead they believe that Fido's responses are conditioned and in fact are ones we have helped create. Some say that the extent of Fido's response is to come running when he hears the refrigerator door open, since food almost always follows and we have conditioned him to this response. But you know what's so strange? When I'm hungry and I hear my wife in the kitchen opening the refrigerator, I come running, too. Either I'm only as intelligent as my dog or my dog is as intelligent as I am in this regard—it depends on how you look at it. Some of these experts insist that only man is capable of putting one and one together and coming up with two, that only man can assess a situation and think out what his response should be. Well, both Tige and I have learned to put one and one together when we hear the refrigerator door open, and we both come running. Sometimes it's a race to the kitchen to see who can get there first. Tige usually beats me.

He's learned to bolt past me with ease, while I slow down or risk falling flat on my derriere. That dog outsmarts me every time.

I believe that dogs are very capable of applying their minds in an array of situations. And the degree of their intelligence can vary from breed to breed and dog to dog—just like people. Here's a case in point.

Years ago, when I was working with dogs in Europe, I witnessed an intelligence test given by some of the foremost trainers and behaviorists in the field. The test involved having various breeds of dog negotiate a high wall in order to get to the other side. Dog after dog jumped over the wall. Finally, it was the standard poodle's turn. The poodle stood there for a moment, as if to size up the obstacle in front of him. Then he casually walked around the wall and joined his fellow canine competitors on the other side of it. These so-called experts concluded that the poodle had failed the test—he hadn't possessed the intelligence to jump over it.

I, on the other hand, concluded that the poodle was the smartest of all the dogs tested. When confronted with this obstacle, he analyzed the situation and chose the easiest way of achieving the goal of getting to the other side of the wall—he simply walked around it! After all, it took a lot less exertion to walk around the obstacle than to jump over it! If that's not thinking, I don't know what is!

And on the homefront, no one conditioned Tige to bang his food dish relentlessly when feeding time is overdue. No one conditioned him to sneak onto my new recliner when I'm not around or to jump off as soon as he hears me approach. He knows he's not allowed—but since he wants to do it anyway, he'll wait until I'm out of the room. The second I return, I'll hear a thump from his leap off the chair, and as I enter the room, I'll find him sitting on the floor ever so angelically. He wasn't conditioned into this behavior. Sure, he knows I don't like him up there, but I definitely didn't condition him to sneak up and then to know when to jump down just before I can catch him. Tige figured that out all on his own. He put two and two together and realized how he could outsmart his pop.

Now before condemning me as some sort of ineffective problem solver, let me say that I could easily stop Tige from jumping
up there. But since he is a basically well-behaved dog, I allow
him a few indiscretions. He knows the score—he knows I don't
like it, but he knows I won't say anything unless he does. It's a
good arrangement and it works for us.

Anyone who's ever taken a high school psychology course
remembers the term "Pavlov's dogs"—a reference to the famous
psychologist's dog-conditioning experiments. It's that very Pav-
lovian theory that has always rubbed me the wrong way, because
it always focuses on animals being conditioned and totally disre-
gards the animals' ability to think. Conditioning is almost always
used for the description of nonhuman behavior, while thinking
and intelligence are almost always reserved for human behavior.

Quite honestly, I wish some of the people with whom I've
done business were as intelligent (and as good natured) as some
of the dogs I've met over the years—and I've worked with
Fortune 500 executives, politicians, celebrities, and highly educated professionals. Believe me, there's a long list of people who
should hope to act half as intelligently as the average dog!

It's not that I disagree with the concept that many animals are
conditioned in their behavior. It's just that I can't understand
man's egotistical philosophy that only we are sufficiently intelligent to actually think and reason. I'll readily agree that humans,
canines, felines, and so forth, are all conditioned in many of their
responses as they go through life. However, if the scientists are
adamant about insisting that only humans think and the rest of
the animal kingdom is conditioned and dependent on instinct,
then I'll do battle with them forever.

If you've ever been owned by a dog, you know what I'm
talking about. Not only can our dogs think, they can actually
master the fine art of human manipulation. Tige, for instance,
has a special look that he reserves only for certain situations.
Now we're all familiar with that alert, ears-pricked-forward-at-
attention, eyes-staring-intently posture our canine companions
assume when they see us eating something—you know, that
"Boy, I'd sure like a piece of that steak" look. Sometimes they'll

even whimper and whine to get our attention. Well, Tige has a special look that he uses only when my mother is visiting. You see, my mom's an even bigger soft touch than I am, and Tige knows it. So he assumes his "Boy, I'd sure like a piece of that steak" look but with a variation. He cocks his head to one side, and somehow—and I don't know how he does it—makes his big brown eyes even bigger and sadder. I call it his poor, forlorn little waif look. You see, Tige knows that this look works every time. The response is always the same. My mom says, "What's the matter with you, Warren? Don't you ever feed him? Come to Grandma, Tigey. My poor, little grandbaby." It doesn't matter that Tige has just been fed and I know there's no way in the world that he could be hungry. He's mastered the fine art of human manipulation, and comes away a winner. You see, my mother marches right to the refrigerator and takes out some tasty morsel for him. Tige wins!

If it's a conditioned response, then why doesn't he use it on me or other people? He saves it for my mother. Tige has put two and two together. Actually, the only conditioned response I see in this whole scenario is my mom's reaction! Don't try to convince me that dogs don't think!

IT'S OKAY TO TALK
TO YOUR DOG

DOGGY DIALOGUE

I think most dog owners will agree with me that Fido and Fluffy do indeed talk to us. It may, however, be hard to convince you that your talking back to your dog is crucial to establishing a strong, healthy relationship with your canine best friend. Even harder yet is convincing those of you who have never been owned by a dog that he'll understand you and appreciate the effort.

By now, I know what you're thinking. "This guy is nuts! Talk to my dog, indeed! Aside from sit, stay, and heel, my dog doesn't or won't understand a word I say."

That couldn't be further from the truth! Look at it this way: Your dog talks to you. He barks, he growls, he whines. He communicates his pleasure when he wags his tail while greeting you at the door or when he licks your face in an obvious show of affection. And what dog hasn't nudged family members under the dinner table in an effort to get a few tasty morsels?

All of these are forms of communication, so why shouldn't

you communicate back? In fact, why not try this: Ask him in your sweetest voice "You wanna go for a walk?" or "Do you want your dinner?" I'll bet you a bag of dog chow that his ears will go up, that he'll cock his head, look you straight in the eye, and even wag his tail in agreement. In fact, many of us have to spell words such as "out," "cookie," and "bath" when conversing with other people, lest we unnecessarily excite our pets. And even then they often understand. I've actually had clients who resorted to using a second language around their dogs, but after awhile their perceptive pooches caught on. Who says dogs don't understand us?

In my twenty-plus-year career in the pet behavior field, I have worked with over forty thousand animals, and I can tell you with absolute certainty that your dog can and will understand you. And I am not alone! My career has enabled me to work with the dogs of many of the world's most famous people. David Letterman's Bob and Stan, Kathie Lee Gifford's bichons frises Chablis and Chardonnay, Phylicia Rashad's German shepherd Nelson, Cheryl Tiegs's wirehair terriers Martini and Olive. The list goes on and on. And, believe it or not, I have had better conversations with these four-footed guys than with some of my two-footed friends! Incidentally, these and other dog owners tell me—and they're not ashamed to admit it—that they talk with their dogs all the time!

So if former first lady Barbara Bush can talk to Millie, and she tells me even George does, there's no reason why you can't talk to your dog. Who knows, your dog may even become a best-selling author as this "first dog" did. It's a fact that Millie's book has outsold former president Ronald Reagan's autobiography!

There are some of you who do talk with your dogs but only in private, because you are afraid your friends and family will label you eccentric. Well, it's time to come out of the closet! Who cares what they think, you're in good company. I'm telling you right here, right now: It's okay to talk to your dog. It's so okay that you should be doing it without feeling the need to hide it. I know other people can make you feel insecure; you may even become the butt of friendly jokes. But ignore these nonbelievers. They're missing out by not opening up to the possibilities of communicating with animals. Just because they won't take off their blinders, don't let them stifle you. You wouldn't let them make fun of you for talking to your kids, would you?

And for those of you who haven't tried it already, it's time to start conversing with your collie and discoursing with your dachshund. After all, your dog is a member of the family and should be treated as such.

Now that I have convinced you that it's okay to talk to your dog, you'll want to know what to discuss with him.

DESTROYING OLD-FASHIONED MISCONCEPTIONS

It wasn't many years ago that dog-talking owners would have been considered the crazy people on the block. Even now, people with old-fashioned misconceptions might still consider you on a par with the local lunatic if you discuss your problems with your canine comrade. But there's no reason in the world not to have an extended conversation with your pet. Go ahead, talk about religion, politics, or the latest joke you heard at work. Many recent medical studies say you just might be better off if you and your pet get into a few heavy conversations. After all my years of being on the doggy dialogue bandwagon, the "prove it to me" scientific community is finally agreeing with me that you could actually end up happier, healthier, and better adjusted emotionally if you talk to your furry companion.

If discussing the latest issue of *The Wall Street Journal* isn't your cup of kibble, at least tell Fido he's a good guy, even if it's for no specific reason. If you're taking a walk and something interesting crosses your path, tell Fido to look at it and ask him what he thinks. Granted, passersby might think you're a wee bit strange (all right, all right—make that a lot strange). But you'll build up Fido's vocabulary and heighten his awareness of things around him.

Yes, I did say build up Fido's vocabulary. You see, I believe dogs have a rather long list of words and even sentences they can understand. Don't be fooled by some experts who say the average canine comprehends ten or twenty words at best. Through a little bit of doggy-dialogue education, Tige has developed some fine language and comprehension.

Speaking of fine language skills, I am reminded of the time I was asked to work with the dog of a member of the Italian diplomatic corps who was based here in the United States. In addition to praising the dog with such standard phrases as "good boy" and "good fella," I had to expand my vocabulary to "bravo" and "bravissimo." Because the dog was bilingual, I had to bone up on my Italian!

Dogs can understand a lot more than a few words, but only if you talk to them. Fido can't learn words just because you think about them. You have to say them, and say them in a way that tells Fido you are talking to him. Take it from me, Fido will try to understand what you're saying. Even the biggest skeptics among you must have seen Fido tilt his head from side to side and wrinkle his furry forehead as he tries to figure out what his human mom and pop are saying.

EXPANDING FIDO'S NATURAL LINES OF COMMUNICATION

All you have to do is take Fido's head-cocking and brow-wrinkling one step further. Talk directly to him, like the real family member he is, not like some lump of Silly Putty on the floor. You'll get out of it what you put into it. By being an intelligent conversationalist, you'll develop an intelligent listener who'll learn to communicate and develop his own dialogue with you.

Dogs all over the world understand that their owners are leaving for the day when they get a kiss and a hug at the door and hear those famous words: "Now you be a good Fido and

take care of the house until Mommy and Daddy get home."
You can see it in your dog's face that he's come to know what
this means. It's his standard good-bye, and he doesn't have to fret
from separation anxiety—he knows you'll be home later because
you told him so. You can almost hear Fido say, "Sure Mom, sure
Pop, no problem. I'll take care of things. I guarantee no burglar
will even try to get near the place." Then off he'll go with a
yawn, ready to embark on a morning snooze, content with the
fact that you told him you'd be back. Those skeptics among you
will say there's absolutely no way Fido knew exactly what we
said. Then at least consider that Fido was reassured by your calm
tone of voice that everything in his life was okay.

DOGS CAN UNDERSTAND

Many of us say good-bye to our dogs. We say good night before
we go to sleep, we ask them if they're hungry and if they need
to go outside. We even ask them what's the matter, if we suspect
they're not feeling very well. Yes, many of us do these things,
and subsequently, our dogs begin to understand some basic
vocabulary. Any animal that has the inherent intelligence to
know when the refrigerator door is open even if he's sleeping in
a second-floor bedroom on the opposite side of the house, and
can then get to the refrigerator faster than a speeding bullet, has
the basic intelligence to comprehend not only simple words but
more than a few complex thoughts as well. The question is:
Does your four-footed best friend want to bother to understand
you, and if so, does he want to let on that he understands? Once
he lets on that he knows what you're saying, there's no turning
back. Fido has tipped his hand. No longer can he stand there and
play dumb when you call him. No longer will he force you to
go to the can opener with his favorite can of food in order to get
his attention. Don't underestimate Fido or Fluffy. They know
what the deal is, but they won't let on unless you help them
develop the art of conversation and make it worth their while.
There are lots of husbands and wives who don't bother doing

much talking and listening to each other, and look what happens to such marriages—they become stagnant and boring. You certainly wouldn't want that to happen to your spousal relationship. Why would you let it happen in your relationship with your dog?

Think of it from Fido's point of view. If all you ever heard was "sit," "stay," and "no," wouldn't you be bored? I am convinced that the overwhelming majority of undesirable behavior in our pets—behavior such as chewing, digging, and general destructiveness—is a result of boredom. But if you actually try to engage your dog in some real conversation, you're going to be surprised. However, don't expect immediate results. There are no fast fixes for relationships that have become so boring that communication has broken down—be it between two people or between an owner and a dog. The longer you and your dog have been involved in a less than exciting relationship, the longer it's going to take to undo the damage. A few weeks probably won't make much of a difference. Give it a few months or more and you'll slowly find that Fido will come around.

You'll know when you've broken through. There will be more eye contact, more close-up-and-personal cuddly situations, and more vocalizing. Listen hard and you'll learn the language. These vocalizations will mean something once you catch on to his lingo. Just keep listening. It's also important to let Fido know that you're trying to understand. Even if you haven't figured out how to translate what he's saying yet, he'll know if you're really making the attempt—and that's what counts. Think of it as a trip to Spain and you don't know a word except "sí." It will be tough, but you'll manage. Both you and the Spaniards will keep at it until you get your point across. As time goes by, you'll learn the language a little at a time. Even though things will be rough around the edges, everyone will understand that you are really trying to communicate. It isn't any different with Fido.

Once Fido understands the basic words, you can even give him a call when you're away from home and leave a message on the answering machine. Tell him you miss him. He'll hear it and know that you still love him. That's what I do for my dog Tige and his kitty comrade Mowdy. You don't know the strange looks I get when I'm at a meeting and excuse myself to call my pets!

If you don't talk to Fluffy, she can't learn. It's as simple as that. If you don't try and don't keep at it, you can't learn, either. Just think of the Spaniards, *"Sí, sí"*!

DOGGY DIALOGUE— HOW YOUR DOG TALKS TO YOU

You don't have to be a pet psychic and you don't need special powers to interpret what Fido says. I believe any owner, if sufficiently interested, can come to understand how Fido speaks and exactly what he is saying. It's easy, and it doesn't require a sixth sense. You only have to learn how to translate the canine language.

For years many humans have thought that we were the only species on Earth that has languages that can be learned and that we alone can communicate with each other. Nothing could be further from the truth. Recently, much work has been done on the complex languages of dolphins, porpoises, and gorillas. I believe that virtually every animal has a language of its own, including man's best friend. Learning how to understand the language of dogs, what I refer to as doggy dialogue, can bring your relationship with Fido to new heights.

The noises that a dog makes, called vocalizations and verbalizations, do not relay worded messages, of course, but they do inform us of Fido's emotional state. Although these vocalizations do not include movement per se, they are part of a dog's body language. Fido's barking could indicate that he is alert, fearful, or protective. The sound of the bark reveals much about what is happening. The so-called normal bark shows alertness, but when the pitch becomes high and shrill, Fido is fearful. A deeper, more resounding bark indicates aggression, and the deeper the growl, the greater the aggression. On the other hand, Fido's growling may be a symbol of a power struggle or an outright declaration of dominance. Whining indicates that Fido is upset. He is not happy about something in the environment. If Fido is yelping, he is probably in pain or has experienced a situation that has shocked him. If Fido is yelping, you should try to determine immediately what's upsetting him. On the other hand, if Fido is squealing, this usually indicates that he is ecstatic or pleasantly surprised.

Fluffy's howling indicates that she either is very lonely or wants to inform pack members that physical or moral support is needed. A howl is usually a signal to gather or rally. Wolves, for example, will howl for entertainment, actually changing pitch in unison while howling. One possible exception is when Fluffy howls at a noise, such as a siren. This is a sign that the sound is bothering her sensitive ears.

And we all have heard a dog sigh at one time or another. A sigh is frequently the finale to Fido's circling, pushing, or scratching out a comfortable position. Sighs most often indicate Fido's contentment, but could also signify a loss of hope. For example, if Fido is left alone, he might howl for a period of time, but upon realizing that no one is returning, he might sigh. If you think about it, this form of verbalization is very similar to what we humans do. I can't tell you how many times my mother sighed after seeing my report cards!

DOGGY DIALOGUE— BODY LANGUAGE

Owners trying to learn doggy dialogue must remember that language isn't just the verbal transmission of actual words. In the case of dogs, it also includes various vocalizations and Fido's nonverbal communication—his body language.

Hundreds of courses and special seminars around the world provide corporate executives and communications majors with the opportunity to learn about human body language. A better understanding of what a person is really saying can give you an edge both in the business world and in day-to-day interaction with people in general. For instance, people sit with their legs either crossed or apart. Some fold their arms or clasp their hands. People interested in each other might cross their legs and move their lower leg and foot. Others might tilt their heads as they listen to conversation. Some make solid eye contact with a person they are talking to, while others dart their eyes around. Experts in human behavior agree that all of these elements of human body language can tell you a lot about another person, whether you're doing business with them or simply conversing.

Since I am convinced that the human animal is not a whole lot different from (or better than) other animals, it follows that dogs have a body language similar to ours. In fact, dogs depend more on body language, whether in the wild or in our homes, than we do. By observing their fellow dogs, and other animals as well, our four-footed friends determine whether they are friend or foe and act accordingly. And they use their own body language regularly to tell another canine what's on their minds.

The way a dog carries his body can tell us so much if we can only learn to translate his language. Is Fido happy, upset, lonely, fearful, content, or surprised? All of these feelings are detectable through his posture and actions. Fido is talking to us with his movements, and we should be ready to hear what he is saying.

FIDO'S BODY LANGUAGE—AGGRESSION

Knowing and reading the signs of aggression are not only valuable for understanding your dog but may help you avoid bodily injury, too. Fido expresses pure aggression in several different degrees. His ears will be pricked or raised and will be obviously forward. If Fido is a breed with hanging ears, the hanging part will be placed as far outward as possible. His lip will be raised around his teeth—the higher it is raised, the greater the degree of aggression. Wrinkles often appear around his nose, and if you were to measure Fido at this time, he would actually be larger. This is due to the fact that the hair on his body rises, his neck arches, and his legs stiffen. His tail will be held high and upright. And the pupils of his eyes may be dilated or enlarged. Your recognition of these telltale signs of aggression will help you to prevent dog bites.

FIDO'S BODY LANGUAGE—FEAR

Fido's feelings of uncertainty, inferiority, or weakness or his reaction to an unpleasant experience will often result in his exhibiting classic fearful tendencies. In many cases his pupils will dilate, his ears will lay back, and the corners of his mouth will be drawn. Fido's face will appear elongated. His tail usually will be held low or between his legs. As owners, we should take positive steps when these symptoms occur. Thorough consideration should be given to rectifying the temperament of any dog that continually displays these tendencies. After all, fearful dogs are often the most unpredictable, and it is not uncommon for a dog to bite out of fear.

FIDO'S BODY LANGUAGE—
PASSIVE AND ACTIVE SUBMISSION

Some of the most classic examples of canine body language occur in the act of what is called passive submission. Submission in canine terms simply means that a dog recognizes that he is not dominant. In other words, he is not the leader of the pack. Passive submission might occur after a dog/owner battle or if Fido has been trained with the old (and I believe harmful) "do it or else" approach. Fido might avoid direct eye contact and pull his lips into a horizontal position. If touched, he may remain perfectly still. He may raise a paw, which should not be confused with an owner-taught handshake. Rather, it is the first sign that Fido is going to lie down and roll over on his back. Urination often follows.

Active submission, on the other hand, is quite different. Although it includes many of the same bodily movements as passive submission, the motivating factor in active submissive behavior is not fear. Instead, it is a demonstration of Fido's acceptance of his subordinate position and usually occurs in positive situations such as the owner's arrival. In active submission, Fido's tongue is usually more extended.

FIDO'S BODY LANGUAGE— THE PLAY DISPLAY

One of the most pleasant and heartwarming exhibitions of body language is the play display. Characteristic of play body language is Fido's tail being held high and wagging, with his front end down and his rear end up. He may play-bite, leap, nudge, or nuzzle with his nose. This is usually followed by a backward jump and a quick charge away from his owner. In essence, Fido is inviting his owner to chase him and enter into Fido's world of play.

DOES FIDO SMILE?

Many people with whose dogs I have worked have said to me, "Warren, I must be going nuts. I am sure that Fido smiles at me." I have to reassure them that they are not losing their sanity. Incredible as it may sound to some of you skeptics out there, some dogs actually do give the appearance of smiling. This is relatively common in dogs with loose facial skin. In fact, I've found that many Doberman owners with whom I have worked have mistaken their dog's smiling for aggression! Most dogs that smile do so when they are playing or when the owner arrives home. Take a close look at the dog who owns you—you'll see I'm not crazy!

FIDO'S WATCHING!

Dogs actually take body language one step further. Most dogs can read an owner's body language and are well aware of when they can play or when they should simply get out of the way and wait until the storm blows over.

Owners are not the only people our dogs study. If your otherwise friendly dog takes an immediate dislike to someone, I suggest you take heed. I'd almost be willing to bet the house that Fluffy's right. Too often I've met people who try to hide their nefarious intentions by acting pleasantly—but they can't fool my Tige. He sees through them, usually faster than I do. In fact, I recently had an insurance salesman come to the house, and Tige took an immediate disliking to him. Needless to say, I didn't buy any insurance from him!

ALL DOGS ARE NOT ALIKE

Before you break out the Berlitz language course on doggy dialogue, it's important to recognize that each dog will have his or her own language variations. While it's true that there are a number of fundamentals that remain unchanged from one dog to another, each dog will set his own tone and have the equivalent of a regional accent. It's best to explain the differences in human terms first. For example, a simple phrase like "that's great" can mean very different things depending on who's saying it and for what reason it is being said. A bubbly, happy-go-lucky type of person would be very sincere and positive when using the phrase, but someone who's a bit depressed or cynical might sneer and mean just the opposite. Said sarcastically, the identical "that's great" takes on just the opposite meaning.

Individual dogs may also have their own innuendos when it comes to communication, and often those innuendos tend to be regional. Now, I'm not saying that this means that Southern dogs say "Woof, y'all" or that tough Bronx street dogs say "Yo-woof!" What I am saying is that dogs from different areas adapt some of the same attitudes as their human counterparts, resulting in differences in language and personality. Dogs living in very hot climates tend to communicate at a slower pace, just like their owners. Their body language is more laid-back; even their vocalizations may be slower in coming. It's simply too hot to be quick in motion and spirit. A case in point: A friend of mine commented on the lackadaisical attitude of the dogs she came across in a small resort town in southern Portugal. She told me that they lie in the middle of the main shopping street, unconcerned about pedestrian traffic. These dogs—not strays, because each is wearing a collar—expect the tourists to step around them while they take their mid-afternoon siestas. Talk about being laid-back!

On the other hand, cold-weather urban dogs are pretty quick to let you know what's going on. The cool weather and fast pace of the city doesn't allow them, or their owners, the luxury of a lot of free time to get their points across. While hot-weather Fido might amble over to let you know it's time for food, his cold-weather city cousin could just about knock you down letting you know that his internal dinner bell is ringing. At the other end of the spectrum, there's rural farm Fido, who has developed all sorts of depth to his communication skills; there's just so much more to relate to as he frolics across the open fields.

TALKATIVE DOGS

In addition to their environments, dogs have different personalities, just as we humans do. Some dogs are the strong, silent type, like Sylvester Stallone, and others are like Joan Rivers—adorable, nonstop talkers. Some owners would give their right arm to have more talkative dogs, and others would give away their homes just to get their dogs to shut up. You know how it is—the grass is always greener on the other side of the dog run.

Several elements help determine the degree to which Fido naturally converses. Sometimes it's genetic—in other words, a simple case of breeding and ancestry, a part of Fido's inherent personality. Many owners of huskies will vouch for this. Other times it is a phenomenon taught by mama dog. A mother's talkative influence sometimes helps create talkative kids. Once again we see that the canine species is no different from the human species! Other canine conversationalists, believe it or not, are created by owners who have come to understand the finer points of animal language. Since breeding and what Fluffy's mama might have done are out of your hands, there's not much you can do about them. However, if you really do want a more vocal best friend, you can learn the basic elements of doggy dialogue and encourage Fluffy to talk more.

As I mentioned before, doggy dialogue takes two forms. To understand Fluffy properly, you'll have to be fluent in both verbal and nonverbal language. To help you along, I've provided some easy tips in the next few sections. Follow them, and eventually you'll be able to understand just what Fluffy is talking about and how you can talk back to her. You can communicate with Fluffy—you just have to know how to go about it.

THE FINE ART OF DOGGY DIALOGUE— VERBALIZATION

By using verbal doggy dialogue, you can have legitimate down-home conversations with your dog. Practice your own woofs and growls and you'll find ones to which your Fido responds. Once you connect with your dog through these verbalizations, you'll have to experiment as to the meanings of the sounds. It's easiest if you try to emulate his sound and tone when he's verbalizing for a particular purpose. Practice a little and he'll catch on—and so will you.

Eye contact between you and your dog, which I will discuss later in this chapter, will enhance any conversation you have with your pet. Fluffy and you will be able to speak very succinctly to each other from opposite sides of the room. I guarantee that, in almost every case, Fluffy will so appreciate the conversation that in no time she'll bound over and leap into your lap for even more personal communication.

TAPE-RECORD FLUFFY

Really nutty dog owners like me get a kick out of tape-recording Fluffy's sounds, making notes as to what was taking place at the time and what she might have been saying. I know, I know—you're thinking, "Now this guy's really lost it!" Just hear me out. After accumulating a few recordings, it's fun and often enlightening to compare these verbalizations. You'll learn that some woofs recorded at different times but under similar circumstances are almost identical and that you were right on target as to what they meant. In other cases you'll learn just how wrong you were, when what you thought were similar woofs are compared. By discovering your mistakes, you'll be able to improve and adjust your language skills. It's a great home research project. When you stop and think about how many years you'll spend with Fluffy, the tape-recording idea isn't as far-fetched as it might sound. If your recording comparisons enhance even one point of communication, it's more than worth the effort.

TAKE IT ONE STEP FURTHER— TAPE-RECORD YOURSELF

Dog owners with a normal interest in understanding their best friends may be content just to understand what they are saying. However, truly devoted, canine-crazy aficionados cannot stop there. We believe that when Fido speaks, it's only fair that we sometimes talk back to him in his own language. You want him to understand English and increase his vocabulary, so continue conversing with him in our language. But if you want to take doggy dialogue to its fullest, try talking to Fido in his own language. He'll appreciate your effort, and you'll see the sparkle in his eyes when you connect. Fair is fair—Fido should learn your language, but you need to make the attempt to learn his, too.

If you really want to go all the way with doggy dialogue, try tape-recording yourself as you practice the various types of woofs. At first you'll probably find there's plenty of room for improvement, but I bet you'll pick up on it. Learning where improvement needs to be made is simple once you hear it on tape. In no time you'll find your stride, and Fido will jump up right alongside you and the tape recorder. He'll know something's going on. As he makes his verbal inquiries, try responding in kind. Before you know it, you and Fido will be engaged in a full-fledged conversation. Don't be embarrassed about mistakes in your grammar or pronunciation—Fido will forgive you!

BODY LANGUAGE

As I said earlier, an important facet of doggy dialogue is body language. It's no accident that Fluffy holds her tail a certain way or cocks her head in an attempt to understand. She can look cute enough to turn your heart to mush or look so ferocious that even

General Schwarzkopf might think twice before picking her up.

Dogs tell us a lot just by the way they carry themselves. Their physical demeanor communicates tremendous amounts of information. In order to better understand Fluffy, it's important to learn this part of her vocabulary. Take Clydie Poops, for example. . . .

Clydie Poops was owned by someone who didn't have a clue as to what he was saying. In fact, Clydie Poops's owner made the typical human assumption of superiority, thereby not even realizing her dog was frequently trying to communicate through body language. But Clydie Poops sure set the record straight.

Clydie Poops's owner began seeing a new male companion, and Clydie Poops didn't like him—no way, no how. At first when the boyfriend came to the house, Clydie Poops just stood his ground, glaring, tail bristling and hackles up. After several weeks, Clydie Poops's behavior progressed—or deteriorated—depending on your point of view. He began to growl—a low, gutteral sound—in the boyfriend's presence. This growl grew louder when Clydie Poops's owner embraced her visitor. Then the big payoff came—the dog lifted his leg on the boyfriend's new Italian leather briefcase. And, needless to say, this did not bring a smile to the boyfriend's face. It did, however, make Clydie Poops's owner laugh. The more she laughed, the more incensed her boyfriend became. Finally he started chasing the dog all over the apartment. He couldn't catch him, and his rage increased to the point where he grabbed an umbrella and took violent swings every time Clydie Poops was in striking distance. Escaping every time, the dog's fleet feet made the boyfriend even crazier. When Clydie Poops's owner sensed that things were getting out of hand, she jumped between the two of them in an effort to break it up. Unable to contain his rage, the boyfriend knocked his girlfriend to the floor. In an instant, Clydie Poops lunged at the boyfriend, his teeth digging into the man's arm, tearing his Ralph Lauren shirtsleeve and drawing blood. The boyfriend wrestled free from the dog and ran from the apartment, his shirtsleeve in tatters, leaving blood droplets all the way down the hall to the elevator.

After the shock of the situation wore off, it dawned on Clydie Poops's owner that the dog was not to blame. Quite the opposite. Clydie Poops had sensed that something was wrong with the boyfriend; he had picked up on things that his owner was too blind to see. The boyfriend's true volatile personality was exposed for the first time when Clydie Poops challenged him.

Clydie Poops had communicated his distrust and dislike through his body language. He had glared at the boyfriend for weeks, had started growling at him, and then had actually urinated on the man's briefcase. Clydie Poops was being very clear as to what he was saying and what he sensed, but his owner wasn't taking the time to really listen to him. Had she paid attention to the way he was speaking to her, she would have realized something was wrong.

I place a lot of confidence in what animals tell me through their body language. If there are any nonbelievers among you, at least consider this: If you have a normally friendly, pleasant dog who generally enjoys everyone's company but takes a dislike to one particular person, take heed. Dogs have an uncanny way of picking up on the innuendos of human personality, behavior, and body language. In the wild, they live or die by their assessments of other animals—so why not the human animal as well? The something extra that Fido picks up on should not be disregarded. You'll often find that Fido knows best.

HOW TO TELL HOW FLUFFY'S FEELING

If you know your dog and you've carefully observed her body language during healthy times, it's easy to observe when something's wrong. When you compare an unhealthy body language to Fluffy's normal happy-go-lucky activities, you don't have to be a pet psychic to sense something is amiss.

How your dog moves or doesn't move certain body parts can tell you how she is feeling or planning to react in the near future. Of course, each dog is different, so the only rule of thumb is:

Owners, know thine own dog, and use the following explanations only as a guide.

THE EYES

Eyes tell me more about an animal I'm working with than any other factor. I believe the eyes are the mirror of the soul. Whether you're doing business over lunch and you need to assess the person sitting across from you, or whether you're dealing with ferocious tigers, a gentle chimpanzee, or the dog in your home, close observation of the eyes will tell you more than a lot of other combined factors. When you're assessing a dog's general behavior, the eyes can be a dead giveaway as to what's coming next.

🐾 *Wide-open Eyes* obviously show Fido's awake, up and around, and alert. Observe the difference between normal wide-open eyes and wide-open eyes that have a mischievous glint. That glint is a dead giveaway that Fido's up to no good. Be aware of that glint and you'll be able to stop that little demon before he gets into any trouble.

🐾 *Half-closed Eyes* mean Fido is relaxed, floating somewhere between being awake and napping. If Fido happens to be on your lap at the time, sort of dozing off, he's showing you that he trusts you to a certain degree. If half-closed eyes occur at times other than when Fido's nodding off, keep your own eyes open for signs of illness. If Fido doesn't feel well, his body language will tell you he's less than bright-eyed and bushy-tailed.

🐾 *Closed Eyes* indicate Fido's asleep or pretty close to it. If he'll allow himself to nod off in your presence, or again on your lap, that's the ultimate vote of confidence. He trusts you implicitly and knows you'd never hurt him.

🐾 *Snoring with Closed Eyes.* What can I say? You lucky devil, Fido's totally relaxed. Ear plugs, anyone?

🐾 *Dilated and Enlarged Pupils Versus Contracted Pupil Slits.* Both enlarged pupils and pupils that seem to close up into small slits can be indicative of pending aggression (see page 22, "Fido's

Body Language—Aggression"). Sometimes the slit reflects a feeling of being threatened (see page 23, "Fido's Body Language—Fear"). Remember, a slit-eyed dog may be forced, by fear, into possible aggression. On the other hand, when a dog is the aggressor, actually initiating the situation, the pupils are usually enlarged or dilated. Either way, these looks should tip you off to a possible aggravated condition that could lead to aggression, complete with growling and biting. In essence, Fido's eyes are saying "handle with care." Be aware of what Fido's eyes are saying, and take a safe approach.

🐾 *Other Circumstances for Slit Eyes and Dilated Pupils.* Just as in humans, Fido's eyes will become slits in order to reduce the amount of light entering the eye so that he can see better. Additionally, the eyes will become slits for better perception of close objects. Conversely, the pupils will dilate to increase the amount of light entering the eye so Fido can see better in low light.

THE MOUTH

Fluffy's mouth speaks for itself . . . no pun intended! It's either relaxed in a comfortable position or displaying some form of open-mouthed, raised-lip warning. Usually, the higher the raised or curled lip, the greater degree of aggression (see "Fido's Body Language—Aggression," page 22). But don't count on this assessment alone. Any curled lip should be taken seriously.

For health reasons, be sure to watch for Fido excessively pawing or rubbing his mouth and face. This is how you may be able to tell if Fido has a toothache, earache, or something in his eye. Remember, the human species can put its discomfort into words; our pets have to rely on body language.

THE EARS

Ears can indicate a pet's mood and purpose. Because they are quite easy to see, the ears are good tools for interpreting body language quickly. An exception is the cropped ears of such breeds as Great Danes and boxers. Ear cropping, the intentional trimming of the ears, results in the perpetual erection of the ears. Needless to say, the resultant constantly alert appearance somewhat reduces the usefulness of the ears as tools for interpreting body language. In such breeds, you can, however, still detect mood, providing you observe carefully.

🐾 *Relaxed but Normally Alert Ears* will move a little, changing direction as they pick up sounds around them.

🐾 *Submissive and Fearful Ears* are usually pulled back, lying flat against the head (see "Fido's Body Language—Fear," page 23, and "Fido's Body Language—Passive and Active Submission," page 23). They're in the perfect position to show another animal that Fido would just as soon give in and let bygones be bygones rather than get involved in an aggressive entanglement. But don't be fooled by submissive ears. If feeling sufficiently challenged, any fearfully submissive animal is capable of shifting gears and attacking for its own self-preservation.

🐾 *Full-blown Aggressive Ears* are usually out of their normal position but not quite flat against the head (see page 22, "Fido's Body Language—Aggression"). They're often somewhat rotated, so that a portion of the back of the ear is almost facing forward. This ear position says, "I'm ready for whatever comes my way and you're not scaring me off!"

🐾 *Twitching Ears* can occur with some dogs at any emotional extreme, whether it be sheer delight, submission, or aggression.

🐾 *When Fluffy Isn't Feeling Well,* she may pull back her ears in various positions, depending on the degree of pain and physical upset. Usually the more pulled back the ears, the greater the pain or upset. Taking it one step further, depending on Fluffy's personality, she may keep to herself (away from you and family members) or stay very close to you when she's upset or uncomfortable. By carefully observing her, you will know if this is occurring, and should take the proper steps to ensure Fluffy's well-being.

THE TAIL

Those of us who are owned by dogs are usually familiar with tails. Haven't we all awakened with one of them in our mouths at one time or another, as Fido snuggled on our pillows? Exceptions, of course, are owners of tail-docked dogs such as Old English sheepdogs and German shorthaired pointers. In the case of these breeds, I always say it's not a good idea to kiss your dog in the dark! But seriously folks, tails have a lot more to do with a dog's behavior than just being the inconvenient body part of a bedtime partner. In fact, I think tails are probably the most misunderstood body part of man's best friend. I wish I had a dollar for every person who's been bitten or attacked by an animal he or she thought was friendly just because the tail was wagging.

🐾 *Happy Tails* can take on a few different postures. One happy tail display is really no display at all: It is neither up nor down, not swooshing or moving, but just hanging there in a casual manner. This is Fido's relaxed mode, when he's feeling pretty comfortable with the world around him.

Tail wagging is often, but not always, a sign of happiness and positive excitement. The key to the preceding sentence is "but not always." You must take in the "big picture," in other words, the appearance of the ears, eyes, and so on, before concluding that Fido's wagging tail is an indication of contentment. Otherwise, you may walk away with a bloody badge of courage!

🐾 *Aggressive Tails* must be recognized. It's important to understand that aggressive tails can also be fearful tails (see "Fido's Body Language—Aggression," page 22, and "Fido's Body Language—Fear," page 23). Remember that the dog, if sufficiently frightened or threatened, might attack. Hence aggressive and frightened tails can have the same body language.

Look out for tails that thump or swing from side to side. Usually the faster and harder the tail moves or thumps, when combined with ears flattened against the head or rotated forward, the greater the degree of aggression. Additionally, a bristling tail held in an upright, arched, or curved position is a fairly obvious sign of the uncertain behavior that could be coming next. The key here is to watch for bristling fur, especially on the neck and back.

🐾 *Submissive and Fearful Tails* are usually held low or between Fido's legs. Here, again, it's important to differentiate between fear and submission by taking in the big picture. Remember, a fearful dog is often an unpredictable dog who might bite out of fear.

Sick dogs will also often hold their tails in a submissive position. Very often, the more submissive the tail position, the greater the illness or pain. Again, only your careful observation of Fido when he is well will enable you to determine if you need to take steps to ensure his well-being.

STRETCHING, YAWNING, AND ROLLING OVER ON THE BACK

Fluffy's stretching, yawning, and rolling over on her back in your presence indicates that she is comfortable enough to be relaxed with you. By exposing her belly, the most vulnerable part of her body, she's saying that she trusts you. This should not, however, be confused with the passive submission position (see "Fido's Body Language—Passive and Active Submission," page 23). Here, again, you must take in the overall situation to differentiate between the two.

I believe Fluffy shows the ultimate indication of trust in her owner when she rolls over on her back, extends her legs out into space, hangs her tongue out of her mouth, and lies in a seemingly catatonic (or should that be dogatonic?) state. It would appear that Fluffy is on another planet (possibly Pluto?). This is, in my opinion, the supreme form of doggy relaxation.

LICKING

All of us who are owned by dogs have been licked by our four-footed friends at one time or another. This can be a sign of affection, a special greeting, an expression of pleasure, or an attention-getting device. On the other hand, Fido may be licking you simply to taste the salt on your skin or the remnants of food you have eaten. So don't flatter yourself!

On a serious note, if Fido develops an obsession with licking a specific spot on his body, it's often his way of telling you there's pain in that area. Be sure you have your vet check it out. If Fido checks out A-OK but continues licking, creating a lick granuloma (an extremely raw area, also called a hot spot), it could be a psychological problem stemming from boredom or stress.

BE A GOOD OBSERVER

Pay attention to Fluffy's body language and you'll be pleased with the results. Not only will you better understand your best friend, but you may be able to pick up early warning signs of illness. Enlisting quick aid from your vet may save Fluffy from serious suffering—or worse. I'm sure you believe Fluffy's worth that much, so attune your eyes and learn how to observe her. Fluffy's giving you all the answers—all you have to do is look.

MAKING DIRECT EYE CONTACT— A MUST FOR A HIGHLY DEVELOPED RELATIONSHIP

I vehemently disagree with all the experts who say you shouldn't make direct eye contact with your pet, particularly sustained contact. While I certainly agree that direct eye contact may not be a good idea with animals who don't know you, as they may interpret it as a threatening gesture, I see no reason to avoid eye contact with your pets. If anything, I believe that direct eye contact can add a new dimension to your relationship.

WHY EYE CONTACT IS SO IMPORTANT

Most dogs (with the exception of the bigger breeds) are small creatures living in a world that's so much larger than they are. Unless they're encouraged to make eye contact, they may never know that your eyes and face are five or six feet up in the air. To prove my point, try this: Lie flat on the floor and have someone stand over you. Strange feeling, isn't it? This gives you an idea of what Fido sees from his perspective. People who are upset, possibly correcting or scolding him, look like tall, over-whelming ogres, scaring him like nothing he's ever known before. Even people who are friendly look something like the Jolly Green Giant. No wonder Fido, especially if he's a smaller breed, is constantly jumping up on you and visitors to your home! He's trying to make contact with a world that towers over him.

I don't think our pet dogs feel as threatened by direct eye contact as they feel uncomfortable. Most of their world revolves around things close to the ground—things that don't include human faces . . . unless you make your face more accessible to Fido.

CRAWL AROUND ON THE FLOOR

Spend more time on the floor with Fluffy. Come on, be a good sport and lie on your belly so that your face is right at her level.

Don't feel silly. It's only right that sometimes you include yourself in Fluffy's physical world. While you're there, encourage her to look at you. Talk to her sweetly and stroke her. Gently place your hands around the sides of her face and position it so that she looks into your eyes. Continue to coo and to talk to her sweetly. At first, if Fluffy is unused to making direct eye contact, she may pull away. Don't force her, just stop and try it again later in the day. Repeat this several times a day for several days. In no time, Fluffy will become more confident about facial and eye contact and will eventually look you straight in the eye. The ability to make direct eye contact will put you one foot (or paw) up on your relationship. As I said before, I believe the eyes are the mirror of the soul. You'll be able to communicate on a level far superior to that of a standard owner/dog relationship. Give it a shot. You and Fluffy will be glad you did.

YOU DON'T HAVE TO BE A PSYCHIC TO UNDERSTAND YOUR DOG

Some people try to characterize what I do (understand what a pet is saying) as the work of a pet psychic, blessed with special powers. Even the Amazing Kreskin, with whom I've had the opportunity to work, said, "Warren, when I see you working with animals, I am convinced you have a sixth sense about them." Well, even the Amazing Kreskin, known for his psychic powers, can be wrong sometimes! I explained to him that I've simply learned to be a good observer. In fact, I prefer, rather, to be described as a modern-day Dr. Doolittle. Although I'm not sure I'm deserving of this flattery, it's the idea of talking to the animals as Dr. Doolittle once did that I most appreciate.

I believe that most of the people who say they have special powers as pet psychics have simply mastered the art of observation. I don't believe that mysterious brain-wave messages are sent from Fido's head to that of the psychic. But I do believe that a person can often interpret the signals of Fido's body language and understand what Fido is saying. Everyone possesses the same basic potential for using their powers of observation. What differentiates some people from others is merely the use and thus the development of the art of observation.

Psychic abilities over and above what I have described may indeed exist. I fully believe there are greater powers than those science has explained—it's just that I haven't yet seen any as they apply to pets. I've been in the same room with some of the most well-known pet psychics and I've yet to be impressed. In fact, in many cases I was actually embarrassed by their incorrect assessments or claims that the correct ones were due to their psychic abilities. I found that by being in the same room at the same time with the same animal and being provided with the same background on each animal, I could better their percentage of correct information simply by observing the animal's various behaviors and taking some educated guesses. You don't have to be a genius or blessed with special mental gifts to understand that a stray dog, after having lived out a good part of his life on the streets, might be timid around strangers. It follows that this dog might be overly possessive of the person who took him in and showed him love and affection. This street dog may have an insatiable appetite as well, now that he has a chance to eat real food rather than meals from garbage pails. There's also a good possibility that he might hate other dogs, since he might have had to fend them off while scratching out an existence on the streets. As I said, it doesn't take a genius to figure it out.

Pet psychics? Go on, give yourself more credit than that. As a loving owner you can learn to understand what your best friend is saying, feeling, and thinking. Keep you eyes and ears open. Take a good, hard look, and keep at it throughout Fido's lifetime. Don't quit after the novelty of that roly-poly puppy wears off. Talking to your four-footed best friend should be an ongoing dialogue. After all, the more you fine-tune your skills, the more information you'll be able to send back and forth. Be patient and you'll see you won't need a crystal ball.

WHY DOES FLUFFY DO THAT?

Every week I field questions from listeners to my Los Angeles and New York radio programs about their dogs' behavior. In the following section I've compiled answers to the most frequently asked questions about our four-footed best friends' behavior.

WHY DOES FLUFFY PANT?

The thousands of sweat glands located all over our bodies enable us to cool ourselves down by sweating. In contrast, dogs only possess efficient sweat glands on their feet. They therefore rely on panting as a means of regulating their body temperatures. If Fluffy begins to overheat, she opens her mouth, extends her tongue, and begins rapid, heavy panting as a cooling mechanism.

WHY DOES FLUFFY RAISE
HER FRONT PAWS?

"Oh, how cute—she wants to shake hands with you!" This is commonly the reaction people have when Fluffy raises her front paw. While this is a sweet notion, it's generally an erroneous one. When Fluffy lifts her front paw, she's often displaying a form of dominant behavior. In doggy society, when one dog meets another dog and raises his paw, he's attempting to establish his dominance over the other dog—so don't flatter yourself!

WHY DOES FIDO ATTACH
HIMSELF TO MY LEG?

Here, again, don't flatter yourself! No, Fido doesn't find you sexually attractive. This is simply another form of dominant behavior. In fact, I'm often asked if Fluffy or Fido is homosexual because they demonstrate such behavior with members of their own sex. My answer has allayed many an owner's worry—this is a display of dominance, not homosexuality.

WHY DO FIDO AND FLUFFY SNIFF
EACH OTHERS' REAR ENDS?

What a lovely topic of discussion—especially at a cocktail party! Actually, every owner at one time or another has wondered about this particular form of greeting exhibited by his four-footed best friend when meeting another dog. While some people theorize that it is sexual in nature, the best explanation

I've heard for this behavior is that it's instinctual, going back to the time when dogs lived in the wild and were constantly on the prowl for their next meal. By sniffing the rear end of another, the dog would get a good idea of what food sources were available in the area.

WHY DOES FLUFFY LICK MY HANDS, FACE, ETC.?

This one also falls in the category of "Look, how cute. Fluffy's kissing you!" While I'm convinced there is an element of affection linked to this behavior, it's more likely that Fluffy's licking your skin for the salt excreted by your sweat glands.

WHY DOES FLUFFY JERK HER LEGS WHILE SHE'S SLEEPING?

Many an owner has glanced over at their sleeping pet and seen her jerk her legs or twitch her feet. Sometimes this jerking motion is so pronounced that owners become alarmed that their beloved Fluffy is having some sort of a seizure. Generally speaking, this "running in her sleep" probably reflects Fluffy's instinct to chase as manifested in her dreams.

WHY DOES FIDO LIKE HAVING HIS CHEST STROKED?

If you're an owner of a male dog, you may have noticed how much he enjoys having his chest rubbed and scratched. Fido finds this particularly pleasurable because it's reminiscent of the sensation he receives during the mating act. You see, when he mounts the female, her back rubs against his chest. I'll bet you'll think twice about scratching Fido's chest the next time!

WHY DOES FLUFFY ROLL IN FILTH?

Some of you have been thrilled to find that while out on a walk Fluffy has flung herself on some foul-smelling mess and rolled over and over in it in an apparent state of ecstasy. It might have been something as aromatic as cow, horse, or deer manure, or even the carcass of a dead animal. The best explanation of this less-than-desirable behavior is that, once again, Fluffy's instincts are taking over. By rolling herself in such a smelly substance, she's camouflaging her own scent with the scent of the prey she'd be stalking if she were in the wild. This practice enabled Fluffy's ancestors to stalk their prey without being detected by the olfactory senses of their intended quarry.

WHY DOES FLUFFY CIRCLE BEFORE LYING DOWN?

Have you ever noticed that Fluffy circles around and around before she lies down? Once again, her instincts are taking over. In the wild, dogs do this to flatten the tall grass in the spot they've chosen to bed down in. It's sort of like how we might fluff our pillows before lying down.

🐾 🐾

WHY DOES FLUFFY EAT GRASS?

Although our four-footed best friends are carnivores, we may on occasion catch them eating grass. There are a couple of theories as to why this occurs. One is that Fluffy is looking for some vitamin or mineral lacking in her diet. Another is that this behavior usually occurs when Fluffy is experiencing some sort of digestive upset. In fact, it's not uncommon for a dog to throw up after ingesting some grass. In some cases it seems to serve as a means of inducing vomiting. Whatever the explanation, if Fluffy suddenly develops this behavior, it's best to speak to her vet to rule out any physical problems.

🐾 🐾

WHY DOES FLUFFY CIRCLE BEFORE AND SCRATCH THE GROUND AFTER DEFECATING?

I think you'll agree that relieving oneself is probably one of the most vulnerable positions you can be in. After all, it's a little difficult to defend yourself with your pants dropped around your ankles! Actually, it's really no different for our four-footed best friends. It is this very vulnerability while in the squatting position that causes our dogs to circle innumerable times prior to "doing their business." By circling, Fluffy can check out the safety of her surroundings—sniffing to see if she detects any potential threats or predators in the area—before she assumes that vulnerable position.

Once she's completed the task at hand, you'll often observe her scratching the ground with her hind legs. This behavior is particularly apparent in male dogs. It is believed that this post-potty ritual is linked to our dogs' instinctive desire to scent-mark their territories. Since their only efficient sweat glands are located on their feet, this scratching serves to deposit their personal scent. I know you're thinking, "Warren, Fluffy's feces are certainly 'aromatic' enough!" Let me assure you that while you can't detect it, this additional scent of sweat *is* detected by the sensitive noses of our four-footed best friends.

WHY DOES FLUFFY CHASE HER TAIL?

If your dog chases her tail, then shame on you! It most likely means that she's bored. Our dogs are incredibly social animals and need constant interaction and stimulation. Puppies, for example, play with, pounce on, and chase their littermates. If a puppy is removed from her littermates and does not receive enough attention from you or enough toys to keep her occupied, she'll make do with the only thing available to her—her tail. That's why you'll see her circling around and around at a dizzying speed in pursuit of her unattainable quarry. In general, you can remedy this by providing her with other outlets for her energy—balls, toys, another puppy playmate, and lots of playtime with you. One word of caution—if your mature dog suddenly develops this behavior, be sure to check his tail area for some sort of skin irritation or impacted anal glands.

DOES FLUFFY SMILE?

I wish I had a dollar for every person who's mistaken a Doberman's smile for a look of aggression! Dogs, like people, have facial muscles that enable them to make an incredible array of facial expressions. Many dogs will curl back their lips, exposing their teeth when they're pleased. And I'm not alone in this observation. In fact, the beautiful white Samoyed of the Arctic is often called the smiling dog of the North. So take a closer look at Fluffy the next time she greets you at the door, and see for yourself!

WHY DOES FLUFFY WAG HER TAIL?

This one also comes under the heading of "I wish I had a dollar for . . ." In this case, it's people who have been bitten by a dog who was wagging her tail. These people operated under the erroneous assumption that a dog who wags her tail is friendly.

"But Warren," you say, "when I come home from work and Fluffy is happy to see me, she wags her tail." Her tail wags, however, not out of happiness but out of excitement. Remember, excitement can be of a positive or negative nature. Of course, your arrival home definitely causes positive excitement. But negative excitement—anxiety or nervousness, for example—also results in tail wagging. In fact, the faster and harder a dog thumps her tail, the greater the degree of anxiety or aggression she is experiencing. In order to determine if a dog is wagging her tail out of distress or delight, it's important to take her entire body language into consideration. For instance, if you observe her ears flattened against her head or rotated forward, or the bristling of the hair on her neck and back, watch out!

FIDO'S MENTAL HEALTH

RECOGNIZING YOUR DOG'S EMOTIONS

In the early 1970s, some of the press had plenty of fun at my expense. Back then, various newspaper and magazine articles referred to me as the world's first pet psychologist—a hound headshrinker and feline Freud. Reporters had a field day as they envisioned a pet lying on the couch, with me sitting alongside listening intently and taking notes. Some drew caricatures. Others set up elaborate photographs with captions proclaiming "America's first psychologist for pets." In the 1980s, according to *People* magazine, I was even spoofed in the movie *Down and Out in Beverly Hills*.

I've never been offended by someone poking fun at what I do. If you're not having a good time when it comes to pets and animals, then it's time to get out of the business. I can say, however, that I have taken great pleasure in having the last laugh. Virtually unheard of in the 1970s, the validity of the field of pet behaviorism is now widely accepted. I'm extremely proud that in the early days I was right out there, in the trenches, espousing my message to anyone who would listen.

Dogs are living, feeling creatures. They laugh. They frown. They can feel upset and stressed as well as lonely and depressed. In essence, I believe pets are fully capable of experiencing the same—or very similar—range of emotions as their human counterparts. While they may not experience them in precisely the same way, they do experience them nonetheless, and to them they're just as real.

Despite the media's comparison, I'm certainly no Sigmund Freud, and I don't believe that a dog owner has to be an expert in psychology in order to recognize Fluffy's various emotional states. However, I do believe problems surface when owners don't acknowledge that Fluffy has mental health needs. Trouble also arises when owners recognize Fluffy's emotional range but don't know what that range includes, what precisely to look for, and what to do if there is an emotional disturbance.

That's why I am devoting an entire section to Fluffy's psyche. Her psyche can be as delicate as she is, but it can also be surprisingly tough. A little bit of knowledge can help you recognize Fluffy's ups and downs, her highs and lows. Best of all, this knowledge will help you detect early warning signs, allowing you to intervene before Fluffy gets in too deep. Mental health is just as important to Fluffy as physical health.

Let's enter the world of modern-day pet behavior analysis.

DOGGY STRESS

Life in industrialized nations has taken its toll on both people and animals. Certainly Fido has felt the demands. He now spends more time alone than ever before, because his family members are working or just plain busy. Just like the concept of latchkey kids, I now see the phenomenon of latchkey pets. Owners come home tired and burned out from working long hours on the job, and Fido senses that. It's easy for him to pick up on the body language of his owners, and in turn react to their tension and stress. Having worked with tens of thousands of dogs and their owners, I am convinced that stress can be transmitted from one end of the leash to the other. By now I know you're thinking, "This guy has really lost it! My dog doesn't feel my stress." Please hear me out: Fido can feel the pressure!

Moving, illness, stays at kennels—and even your marital problems can affect man's best friend. So think twice before you argue in front of Fido. Does he really need the extra stress in his life? He sure doesn't—and neither do you. Take a couple of deep breaths, count to ten, and forget about it—if not for your own sake, at least for Fido's!

MENTAL STIMULATION FOR GOOD MENTAL HEALTH

I bet you've never given your dog's mental health much thought. Well, throughout this book you'll find many references to the fact that dogs are intelligent, perceptive, and emotional creatures. You'll also find me on a perpetual bandwagon exhorting the need for owners to pay more attention to keeping Fluffy's mind active. As there is virtually no one talking about this crucial area of canine care, I feel I need to keep driving home the point. Inactive minds can contribute to the development of many undesirable negative behavior habits and can create unhealthy mental attitudes that can take their toll on Fluffy's physical well-being. I firmly believe that the body works as a unit. In other words, both physical and mental health play equal supporting roles to make up the whole.

There are numerous studies demonstrating that psychological stress can weaken a human's ability to stave off illness and disease. I'm thoroughly convinced the same holds true for Fluffy. I am also convinced that most dog owners do not pay nearly enough attention to their four-footed best friends' frame of mind. It's not that these people are cruel or abusive, it's just that no one ever points out Fluffy's need for good mental health. The fact of the matter is that many of today's dogs are kept indoors virtually all of the time. Except for two or three brief walks a day, they spend hours on end in homes where everyone works or is out of the house all day. Some of the smaller breeds have actually been litter-box or paper-trained, thus eliminating the need for even those brief outings.

Let's take a look at how the typical dog in this situation spends his day: sleeping late into the morning, then taking an even later morning nap, then napping in the early afternoon and again in the late afternoon. In between snoozing, there's a little aimless wandering around the house. With the exception of one or two meals, two or three hurried walks, and possibly some barking at the mailman or delivery boy, there's not much to do. With nothing to do but watch soap operas all day, I'd chew on the Chippendale chair myself!

That's basically what happened with two former clients of mine, David Letterman's dogs Bob and Stan. Dave's grueling schedule with his then new television show meant that Bob and Stan spent a lot of time alone. Dave's new job had required a move from the open spaces of Malibu, California, to the confinement of a New York City apartment. These two factors helped aggravate some aggressive behavioral problems. It was apparent that life in the Big Apple didn't hold a candle to Bob and Stan's old beachfront playground, and that had a negative effect on their psychological well-being. By analyzing the situation, I was able to come up with the proper resolution.

DON'T MISS THE CHANCE TO DO ONE OF THE MOST IMPORTANT THINGS YOU CAN DO FOR YOUR DOG

As you read through this book, you'll find that I've included several chapters that deal specifically with psychological problems. I've also included dozens of suggestions about things you can do to keep Fido on his toes, properly stimulated, and less stressed—all of which will help keep him both physically and mentally healthy and sharp.

The key to Fido's good mental health is the use of mental stimulation. Don't be lulled into thinking that everything's okay with your dog. Think about a party or a picnic for Fido. Spice up his life and you'll probably be surprised by the changes you see. The majority of my clients don't realize their dogs need anything more than normal affection, but once they get started on my program, they notice a lot of subtle changes in Fido's behavior. He demonstrates increased vigor and enthusiasm accompanied by a healthy glow. As a result of the combination of all these small improvements, the dog turns into a very different canine, one that's certainly better off for your efforts.

DOGGY DEPRESSION— IS IT REAL OR ARE WE CRAZY?

Can man's best friend become depressed? Will Fido need to curl up next to his own personal Valium bottle? Does he need couch sessions with a pet shrink to straighten out his head?

Controversy rages over whether dogs have the emotional capacity to become depressed. People with opinions on both sides of the question engage in heated debates. Believers in doggy depression say, "Of course dogs become depressed. Just look at their behavior." But nonbelievers argue that the thought of dogs having the emotional capacity for depression is anthropomorphic. They say dog lovers, as with all animal fanatics, just attribute human behavior to their pets. As far as nonbelievers are concerned, it is the owners, not their dogs, who are emotionally unstable, since they think of animals in human terms. Both sides argue their points with unwavering conviction.

When you get down to it, the disagreement centers on new behavioral theories, pets' emotional capabilities, and on how they interact within families. With any new idea, there are always going to be skeptics. I believe anyone who has had a close relationship with a dog knows unequivocally that a dog can become depressed. I am convinced that anyone taking the opposite point of view has spent too much time in the laboratory, testing his own theories, and not nearly enough time on his hands and knees building a special relationship with a dog.

I've seen many pets mourn their deceased masters. So often widows have told me how their dogs have waited at the front door for "Daddy" to come home from work at night—months after Daddy has been laid to rest. You have no idea how many times my clients' owners have contacted me because Fido has turned lethargic, wandering all over the house looking for Junior after he's moved out to go to college or for a companion pet who has gotten lost or passed away. Divorce, which is unfortunately all too commonplace in our society, also plays a big part in creating depressed dogs. They don't understand the arguments and general upheaval that normally accompany a divorce. They surely don't understand when, suddenly, family members and even the kids disappear.

Depression brought about by mourning or a feeling of abandonment is very upsetting to Fluffy—you can see the pain in her eyes. It breaks your heart that she's so terribly confused—you wish you could explain it to her in terms she could understand. Fortunately, tender loving care helps most pets out of this type of temporary depression—just as it helps humans who find themselves in this condition. The pitfall here is that very often the owner is suffering through similar personal problems relating to a family member's death, a divorce, or the empty nest syndrome. While busy trying to cope with their own problems, owners often forget that Fluffy needs a different, more caring type of attention during the same period of time. She needs to be soothed when there's so much emotional upheaval going on, and she desperately needs compassion. Owners, please be aware of your dog's needs during these tough times. I realize that it's hard to think of your dog when your life has just been torn apart, but sharing your grief with Fluffy will certainly help her. And it will more than likely help you, too. Snuggling a dog makes us all feel better.

I know firsthand the benefits and comfort derived from sharing grief with pets. After my wife passed away from a long illness, I hated returning to the house we had shared for many years during our marriage. The only thing that forced me to go back inside was the knowledge that my dog Tige and his kitty comrade Mowdy were waiting for me. They depended on me—for both food and moral support. One of the hardest things I've ever done was to enter that house and tell them that "Mom" wouldn't be coming back home ever again. That night all three of us grieved together.

Tige and Mowdy had known that something was up. For several weeks I had been at the hospital for long periods of time, making it necessary for me to count on the kindness of family and friends to feed and exercise my four-footed friends. Tige and Mowdy sensed that something was wrong. They missed me and they missed their Mom. How could I explain to them what was going on? Yet they knew. On the evening I returned to that empty house, they consoled me as much as I consoled them. We depended on each other. And that dependence has never stopped. There were days that I did not want to go on, but knowing that Tige and Mowdy needed me—were counting on me—*made* me go on. Yes, it's important to help our pets over such rough times, and they, in turn, will help us.

Divorce, the death of a friend or family member, or the kids going off to college are obvious causes of depression. Because of the abrupt change in Fluffy's life, these causes are usually easy to recognize. But are you astute enough to recognize the type of depression that may be killing off your dog a little at a time? Does the following scenario sound familiar?

You've been very busy for more days or weeks than you care to recall. It seems there just isn't enough time in the day. The dog gets underfoot, dragging out her favorite ball in a vain attempt to get you to play with her. You've got a million and one things to do. You trip over the ball and yell at Fluffy. She pulls back her ears and runs to hide under the nearest piece of furniture. Resting her head on the floor, she watches every move you make with big bulging eyes. She's hoping for just a few minutes of your time. You just don't have a moment to spare. There's too much work to be done, too many errands to run. You feel bad, so you promise yourself that you'll find some time tomorrow to play with her and give her plenty of special attention. But tomorrow comes and you're still busy. Fluffy feels as if she's being treated as part of the furniture. The next day is no different—you're still too busy. Finally, the following day, you take the time to play, and even cook her favorite chicken dinner. You both have a grand old time, but the next three weeks come and go and you're very busy again. Haven't you noticed by now that sweet little Fluffy is withering away?

Neglect is the number one cause of depression in our pets. It happens so gradually, most of us don't see it coming. Then, all of a sudden, Fluffy looks old. It sneaks up so slowly until one day you realize what you've done (or haven't done) and the effect it's had on your best friend.

That's exactly what happened to Brandy. At three years old she was a gorgeous golden retriever. Brandy was owned by a successful young couple—he was a junior partner at a prestigious law firm, she was an agent with an aggressive real estate company specializing in million-dollar-plus properties. In order to climb their respective corporate ladders, they worked excruciatingly long, hard hours. Since having a child at that particular point in their lives would hamper their careers, they opted for a dog on which to lavish their affection. Deciding to be good Samaritans, they went to the local animal shelter and adopted Brandy.

Her allotted time at the shelter had been almost up, with no potential adopters in sight. Brandy lucked out in that respect. She was plucked from the shelter only hours before she was scheduled to be euthanized.

In the beginning, everything was terrific. With plenty of attention, love, and affection, Brandy thrived. She was perky and playful and very adorable. Her mistress even left the office a little earlier or stopped home in between appointments to make sure Brandy was okay. Since it was a new environment, Brandy's owners didn't want her to get too lonely.

Because everything was going along so beautifully, it was easy for Brandy's owners to get lulled back into their old work habits—long hours and taking work home. Their dinners usually consisted of Chinese takeout or pizza. After all, who had the time to shop, let alone cook a meal? Sometimes even Brandy's food ran low, so out of convenience and sheer exhaustion her owners would create makeshift meals of ground beef, even beef with broccoli. It reached the point where Brandy wasn't happy even with these special meals because she didn't like eating by herself. It was lonely eating in the kitchen while everyone else ate in bed watching TV. Starved for attention, Brandy opted to stay in the bedroom with her owners, leaving her food untouched in the kitchen. Food took a backseat to companionship, and lots of leftover dog meals were thrown into the garbage.

Brandy seemed bored and started sleeping more. Since it was wintertime, her owners attributed her inactivity to the season and figured things would change come spring. Brandy developed a little cough at night. Suffering from allergies themselves, Brandy's owners assumed her coughing was nothing serious. They were so tired, sleeping like logs, they didn't hear Brandy, anyway. Brandy's coat became dull and dry, but they figured that was due to the drying effects of their apartment's steam heat. She looked a little thin around the ribs, but they convinced themselves that because her coat was so dry it wasn't really her weight that was a problem—it was just an illusion created by her less dense coat. However, they decided they'd take her to a vet anyway. They set up an appointment but had to cancel it because of a late business dinner. They promised the receptionist they'd reschedule soon, but they didn't get around to it.

One day when they came home, Brandy wasn't at the door to greet them. She was lying on the bed barely able to move. They rushed her over to the vet, but it was too late. Brandy didn't last out the night. Worst of all, she died in pain. Dear, sweet Brandy, what did they do to you?

Did depression kill Brandy? No, not quite. However, it is a question of which came first, the chicken or the egg? The point of this sad story is that when there is any problem with your dog's mental health, particularly depression, many other important things become affected—diet and exercise are certainly two of them. As Fluffy becomes a poor eater and spends less time exercising in the fresh air, her immune system gets progressively weaker. When her immune system weakens, Fluffy is a prime target for almost any bacteria or viral infection that comes her way.

THE SIGNS OF DOGGY DEPRESSION—WHAT TO LOOK FOR

The best way to know when something's wrong is to pay close attention to your dog's behavior when everything's right.

- Note how much Fido normally plays so you'll be able to know when he develops an unenthusiastic attitude toward the toys and games that once amused him.

- How's his normal appetite? Has he always been finicky, is he moderately picky, or does he always gobble up his food? Depressed dogs often go off their feed, much in the same way that a depressed person loses his or her appetite. Conversely, a picky eater may suddenly become a nervous eater, the same way some people binge when they're down in the dumps. Any change in appetite is a good clue for the assessment of depression, particularly if your vet has given Fido a clean bill of health.

- Note your dog's sleeping habits. Nine times out of ten, depression is accompanied by signs of general inactivity. Depressed dogs tend to lounge around the house and do much less than dogs who are in a good frame of mind.

- Be on the lookout for changes in behavior. Is the normally mellow dog more aggressive, or is the normally very friendly, sociable dog keeping to himself, even when company drops in? Any real change in behavior can be an indication of a much deeper problem.

- Take a good look at Fido's eyes. Do they still reflect life's excitement, or is the sparkle gone? The eyes will let you know how your dog is feeling.

- Finally, take a picture of your dog when things are going right. This way you'll have something to refer to in the future. Six months or a year from now you can take out the picture and make a comparison. If you currently suspect something is not right, try to find a picture of your dog taken a year ago. Of course, he'll look a little older, but you might detect something else. Take a good look at the eyes. Are they as happy to be alive as they were in the photo? If your answer is no, it's time to take immediate action.

TRICKS FOR LIFTING YOUR DOG FROM THE DEPTHS OF DEPRESSION

Recognizing that your best friend is depressed is the important first step. Knowing how to lift your dog from that depressed state comes next. If you've been able to assess the damage and determine what might have triggered the problem, you're definitely ahead of the game. Perhaps you can find a replacement for the loss of whatever caused Fluffy to become depressed in the first place. For example, if Fluffy suffered the death of her canine companion, you may find that adding a playful puppy or kitten to your household is the solution. Or, if you can't commit to another full-time pet, why not throw several parties for your dog and invite some of her canine comrades over for a change? "My dog doesn't have any friends," you say. Then shame on you! Dogs definitely need a few friends of their own. It's time for you to expand Fluffy's social calendar and develop a new circle of canine companions. How about inviting over some of the other dogs Fluffy regularly sees on her walks? Just be sure she and all the invited guests get along well with other animals. And if your dog was used to a lot of household activity—the kids coming in and out of the house with their friends, for example—and now things are quiet, it's time to repay some of those dinner invitations you owe. Throw a few dinner parties and luncheons, for humans this time, in order to create more dog-human interaction. And for heaven's sake, don't lock Fluffy in the other room while you're entertaining! The whole point is to get Fluffy to mingle and interact. If you're thinking, "I can't have her around when company comes—she'll jump on everyone and make a nuisance of herself begging for food," you'll just have to read my chapter on manners (see the section that begins on page 170).

It's not always easy to figure out what causes Fluffy's low spirits. Often a really depressed state comes about from a combination of factors, not simply one isolated reason. If this is the case, my preferred plan of action is a well-varied program for perking up Fluffy's life.

CHANGING THAT HO-HUM ROUTINE

The best way to put the zip back into a dull daily existence is to make some changes. Mix things up a little. Dogs who don't quite know what to expect will begin to look forward to the uncertainties of the next day. Try cooking something special once a week or so and adding a little bit of it to your dog's regular food—just enough to add a little flavor. Tige always gets excited when he sees me cooking spaghetti because he knows he'll be getting a little bit of Parmesan cheese sprinkled on his kibble. Buy lots of new toys and put most of the old ones away for another day. Remember, variety is the spice of life! Why not try a little doggy massage (see page 203) or a doggy makeover (see page 247)? And be sure to get your best friend out of the house. No, his regular walks don't count. If I passed the same fire hydrant day in and day out, I'd be depressed, too! Go somewhere different—a different park or a different neighborhood. How about a visit to Grandma or the nieces and nephews? Odds are he will love these special excursions, returning home happy and content afterward.

Owners, please treat your dog's depression like the serious, real problem it is. An emotional valley, if left unchecked, can be as threatening to a dog's health and happiness as many other "real" medical problems. If you believe your dog is depressed, don't let your friends and family embarrass you out of acting by suggesting that you're the one with the mental problem. Your dog is counting on you! As I've said before, dogs are intelligent, sensitive animals and are just as capable of experiencing a wide range of emotions as humans. It's up to you to support the emotional needs of your beloved four-footed best friend.

LATCHKEY DOGS LEFT ALONE ALL DAY

You're probably asking yourself, "What in heaven's name is a latchkey dog?" Latchkey dogs, like latchkey kids, are left alone and to their own devices while the adults are at work or out of the house running errands and doing chores. The phrase latchkey kid was coined when women with children joined the work force in droves. Their kids would come home from school, unlock the latches or locks with their own set of keys, and let themselves into an empty house, where they remained until the adults returned from work later that afternoon or evening.

Latchkey dog is a phrase I coined soon after the advent of latchkey kids. Although Fido's not actually struggling with a set of keys scrunched between his little paws trying to let himself in, the concept is basically the same. With the proliferation of two-income households, households headed by a single parent, or even in the plain old single household, mothers just aren't around the way they used to be when I was growing up. No, this is not intended to be a chauvinistic statement—it's simply a statement of fact. Nowadays, even if Mom doesn't work, she's usually running around doing dozens of family errands during the day. Regardless of what type of household Fido lives in, odds are he is left alone a lot of the time.

What does being a latchkey pet mean to your dog? It means being alone probably eight to ten hours a day while you work; being alone another hour or two while you shop or go out to dinner, and alone again another eight hours while you sleep. Add it up and what do you get? A dog that's left unattended anywhere from sixteen to twenty hours out of every twenty-four-hour day. That's a lot of time in solitary confinement!

ARE WE ASKING TOO MUCH—
SHOULD A DOG BE A LATCHKEY DOG?

If you're a member of a working or busy family, or if you live a busy single lifestyle, is it fair to own a dog? That's a good question to ask based on the above figures. The answer is "yes," as long as you bear one very important point in mind—quality time is more important than quantity time. It's just like having kids. One mother might be home all day long and ignore her kids. She might never ask them what they learned in school today or if they have any homework to do. Another mother might work all day outside the home, yet upon returning home at the end of the day, she'll help her kids with their homework and class projects. Whose kids do you think will do better in school?

ARE YOU FEELING GUILTY ABOUT LEAVING
FLUFFY ALONE,
OR THINKING ABOUT FINDING HER A NEW
HOME?

Don't give up on your best friend! I know the figures I quoted earlier may seem overwhelming, but there's no guarantee that the next home will be a loving one. Sometimes spending minutes with someone you love is more important than spending hours with someone you don't.

WHAT YOU CAN DO TO BE FAIR
TO YOUR LATCHKEY DOG

Each day, find a few special moments to spend with your best friend. Don't be a weekend parent and overdo things on Saturday and Sunday to make up for lost weekday time.

So that Fido has something to do while you're out, take some of his favorite treats and hide them where he won't find them too easily but will be able to locate them eventually. As he wanders aimlessly around the house during the day, he'll come across a little surprise here and there. It will go a long way in helping perk up his day and might even take his mind off that day's decision of whether to chew up the new couch or leave little presents all over your Oriental rug. Remember, adding the element of surprise is an ideal way to mix up Fido's ho-hum daily routine.

If you are concerned that leaving small food treats around the house will attract unwanted guests—namely insects—to your home, consider buying an automatic feeder. Its timer can be set to uncover his food dish at appointed hours, so Fido always has a little nosh to break up the day. I prefer the battery-operated ones, so Fido doesn't have electrical cords close to where he's snacking. Some newer versions can be set to open several times during the day and to close gently so he can't be hurt. The noise that accompanies the opening of the cover is enough to let him know it's snack time. If Fido's food has the tendency to spoil, seek out an automatic feeder that comes with ice packs that can be placed under the food dish to keep the contents properly chilled. Your best friend can then have his own little party even when no one's home. Now, what more could you, or he, ask for?

When you do come home, spend the first ten minutes or so with your dog. He'll be excited and all charged up to have someone around. If you don't give him some positive attention upon your arrival, be prepared to deal with his stored-up, misguided energy all night long. If he's really craving attention, he may even work his way into what I call a negative attention syndrome. Fido knows he's going to be yelled at but opts for negative, corrective attention rather than no attention at all. As I've said before, our canine family members aren't much different than our kids. So, in those first ten minutes when you walk in the door, no matter how tired you are, play a little game that he enjoys, then give him a few minutes of loving and hugging. He'll be better behaved the rest of the night, and it will actually take less of your time than if you have to constantly interrupt what you're doing to chase after and scold him as he desperately tries to get a reaction out of you.

At least two or three times a week, preferably more if you can, get Fido out of the house. Remember, his regular walks for the purpose of elimination don't count. How about a special outing to his favorite park or a Little League game? Take him to see some of his canine comrades. Anything! Just do something. I promise you, Fido's not fussy. He'll be grateful for any time away from the house. It will break up his monotonous routine and keep those same old four walls from closing in on him. If you work in a small office, perhaps you can take him to your job once in a while. If not, find ways to work him into your schedule. It won't take you any more time to bring Fido along on a quick trip to the drive-through store. And since it's a drive-through, you won't have to leave him unattended in the car.

Remember to experiment with calling Fluffy on the phone and leaving a message on your answering machine. I know it sounds eccentric, and heaven forbid me being called eccentric! But some dogs love to hear your voice and know that Daddy and Mommy is talking to them, while others are frustrated if they hear you but can't find you. That's why it's important to experiment. I can tell you that Tige loves it. It's especially reassuring to him to hear my voice when I'm out of town overnight on business. Even when I'm out only for a few hours, I let him know that Daddy will be home soon and we're going to play chase, his favorite game. He knows that, as soon as I come home, we'll chase each other around the living room table. Of course, as always, he'll win. But that's okay, he's got the advantage of having four legs.

If leaving a message on the answering machine doesn't work for you and your dog, try leaving a radio on that is set to a talk station. The voices may help Fluffy get through the day. At least it'll keep her company, and she'll be able to give you the latest stock quotations.

Some dogs like to hear a recorded family conversation that has been taped on a continuous-play cassette. This way Fluffy has the comfort of the family's voices around her all day long. Just as with the answering machine, you'll have to experiment to see if it helps or if it frustrates her because she can't find you in the house.

Get up ten minutes early and provide Fluffy with some special playtime. If we expect our dogs to be good all day long, the least we can do is set the alarm clock a little bit earlier than normal. Yes, I know it's hard to get up earlier than you have to. You may even take the step of setting the alarm clock a few minutes earlier, then be tempted to push the snooze button when it goes off. Make the effort! After all, if you honestly—and I mean honestly—can't find an extra ten minutes in the morning to spend with Fluffy before leaving for work, you should consider whether you have the time and proper attitude to own a dog in the first place.

Say good-bye when you leave the house. Have a little conversation as you head for the door. You know the kind: "You be a good girl. Watch the house while I'm gone. I'll see you this evening." Some people say you should just leave and not make a big production out of it, but I couldn't disagree more. How would you feel if your husband or wife just left the house without saying good-bye? I think it's very important to give Tige a special good-bye in the morning. We have a private little hug and smooch, then I tell him I'll be back later and that he should be a good boy. He's come to know the routine, and I know he finds the good-bye and personal contact very reassuring.

Say hello when you come home. Tige always greets me at the

door the instant I arrive home. It's adorable to see Tige and his feline brother, Mowdy, sitting alongside each other just waiting to say hi. Together they act like my personal welcoming committee. So when your furry fan club runs to the door to greet you, put down your packages and the dry cleaning and give your four-legged friends the type of greeting they're giving you. It only takes thirty seconds, and I guarantee it means a lot to them.

Think about getting a pet pal for Fido. A cat or dog friend may just be what he needs to pass the time (see page 69 for information on how to introduce a new pet into the house).

Latchkey dogs are a special breed. At no other time in the history of man have pets been asked to stay cooped up and alone for so much of their lives. We're asking a lot of our dogs to put up with our modern lifestyle. The least we can do is try to meet them halfway. It's only fair. It's only reasonable. And it's the only humane thing to do.

FIDO'S MIDLIFE CRISIS

Please try to control your laughter and hear me out on this one. There comes a point in some dog owners' lives when the thrill is gone and the novelty of having a dog in the house has worn off. After all it took for Fido and owner to settle in with each other—the house-breaking, the obedience training—you'd think they could just sit back and enjoy the meeting of the minds for years to come. You know what I mean—Dad sitting by the fireplace in his favorite easy chair with his middle-aged, happy hound curled up at his feet. Well, I hate to break the bad news to you, but it ain't necessarily so. The key words here are "middle-aged" and "happy." Unfortunately, these words don't always go together. Often what happens is that Fido gets taken for granted. It's kind of like a comfortable old pair of slippers that fit perfectly—why bother looking for anything else, even though they're worn, dirty, and need a change?

I'm sure you've all heard of people who have gone through

midlife crises. They've spent many years doing things they're not so certain were right for them. Sometimes a midlife crisis results in a few simple changes—a different hair color or style, a new wardrobe, a new job. These are all minor changes. On the other hand, sometimes it results in a lot more than that. There may be a change in spouse or relocation to a new city. In any event, midlife often means a need to reinvigorate the mind and the body.

Can Fido have a midlife crisis? You bet he can—particularly if his life has become one big routine lacking in things to keep him interested and alert. He can become bored, depressed, inactive, experience a personality shift, or undergo almost any psychological or physical change you might expect from a human being going through midlife difficulties.

Now that you're done laughing and understand that even man's best friend can find himself in a midlife rut, just what should you do about it?

Well, Fido can't dye his hair or go on a shopping spree. The best approach, of course, is to prevent a midlife crisis from happening in the first place. It won't happen at all if you apply all the information in this book and keep Fido mentally and physically stimulated throughout his lifetime. Don't let him take a backseat to what goes on in your life. Dogs who get pushed aside because of owners' busy lifestyles are in the greatest jeopardy. However, dogs owned by people who have fallen into their own monotonous daily routines are equally at risk. It's possible for an owner to be home with Fido all day long and still not provide the type and quality of attention that's required.

If you suspect a midlife problem is affecting your dog, the resolution is similar to the steps I described earlier for resolving depression: Change things around. Make everything a little different. Different food, excursions to different places, even a different wardrobe. Yes, I did say a different wardrobe! Go shopping for a new leash or a new collar. How about a new sweater or raincoat? And while you're at it, how about some new toys? Develop a canine toy chest, even if you think he won't play with toys anymore. You just might be surprised by his interest in his new playthings. At the very least, he'll appreciate your effort. Go out of your way. A little extra TLC will keep Fido emotionally happy, and may even help him live a physically happier life. Just as with people, active happy dogs don't get sick as often as listless ones. Pay attention to Fido's mind—it will serve both of you well.

Owners of young puppies, remember this chapter a few years from now. I know it's hard to believe it—right now you're spending so much of your time nuturing your four-legged best friend—but some day you may need it. Owners of middle-aged dogs, it's time to get a move on it. Maybe your dog is not as cute as he was as a puppy, and maybe he doesn't appear to be as demanding of your attention as when he was younger. Don't take him for granted. What you do today can make a big difference in Fido's vitality in the years to come.

DO DOGS CRY EMOTIONAL TEARS?

This is a hot topic. Although there are many claims in support of this theory, the scientific community is skeptical about animals crying emotional tears. Hard evidence doesn't really exist, but there's so much anecdotal evidence that it cannot be overlooked.

It may be that not all animals cry emotional tears, but there's a likelihood that some do. Dian Fossey, the late gorilla expert whose life was documented in the movie *Gorillas in the Mist*, related a story about seeing Coco, one of her prized gorillas, cry for emotional reasons. Of the many gorillas Fossey worked with over the years, Coco's was the only such case, but this well-respected animal expert swore it happened.

Even Charles Darwin wrote an account of elephants shedding emotional tears. On the other hand, many zookeepers and similar experts emphatically state that they have never seen an animal cry for emotional reasons. The animals' eyes may have watered and shed tears, they say, due to various physical irritants such as dust or pollen, but not due to an emotional upset. Now that you've read the preceding sentence, I would like you to consider something I once read about the director of one of the world's most famous zoos. It concerned a case of alleged animal abuse in his facility. I was shocked to read that he felt that the charge of abuse was unfounded—he felt that tying down an animal while several trainers and handlers beat it about the head and body was an appropriate method for dealing with an uncooperative animal. The account concluded with him stating something to the effect that it was, after all, just an animal.

Well, if this is the type of mentality that is responding to the question of whether animals shed emotional tears or not, is it any surprise that the answer is negative? As far as I'm concerned, this type of person wouldn't know an emotional tear if it dripped onto his face.

Can animals cry? A couple of years ago I received a letter from a child who said that whenever she cried, her cat Muffy would cry with her. The little girl's parents ignored the story until one day after she had been punished the parents walked into her room and found two wet pillows and two wet faces.

I've asked this question of the audiences of my radio shows, and much to even my surprise, amazing numbers of pet owners swear they have had similar experiences. Most of these cases seem to involve the loss of a family member or another family pet.

Although I've owned many dogs in my day, I personally have never seen emotional tears in any of them. But now that I think about it, the night I came home and told Tige and his kitty comrade Mowdy that their Mom wouldn't be returning, they might have cried. It was hard for me to see; after all, I had tears in my eyes.

FIRST-DOG PSYCHOLOGY—HOW TO INTRODUCE A SECOND PET TO YOUR DOG

AVOIDING FIGHTS

The third most frequently asked question appearing in my monthly mailbag of a thousand-plus letters is what to do about fighting between pets who live in the same household. If you guessed that pets leaving little accidents and presents all over the floor is the number one problem, you're right. Also correct is a guess that the second most frequently asked question has to do with pets redecorating and redesigning the landscape—both inside and outside your home—by chewing and digging. But how many people would suspect that the number three problem on the minds of those of us who are owned by dogs is the battle between canines? (Important note: Owners wanting to know about dogs getting along with cats, birds, and other animals should read further. The advice in this chapter can be applied to your version of the problem as well.)

Problems range from mild-mannered mongrels who turn into furious fireballs of nastiness when another dog enters the picture to dogs who tolerate each other but periodically have serious knock-down-drag-out fights. There are also the James Dean–type doggies who seem to be okay on the surface—but on a deeper level you can tell there's something brewing. It's just a matter of time before there's a blowup.

How come there are so many fighting dogs these days? Why does the fur fly, and why, suddenly, has this become an issue at the forefront of dog ownership? The answer is three-fold: First, dog owners are wild about dogs! There are a lot of dog-loving people who open their hearts and homes to a number of dogs.

Second, dog lovers are animal lovers, and that means they are opening their homes to all types of God's creatures. For instance, statistics show that the cat population has increased dramatically over the last few decades. In fact, cats now outnumber dogs as family pets. It therefore follows that there are an increasing number of multipet families. After all, our feelings of guilt for leaving Fido alone all day—his becoming the latchkey dog I described earlier in this chapter—lead us to seek out additional companions for him. The final factor contributing to an increase in aggressive behavior among our dogs is related to this same latchkey syndrome. With human household members absent from the home for such great periods of time, there's bound to be competition among pets for the family's limited attention.

Visions of two or more dogs living happily ever after are often shattered when the pets take an instant dislike to each other. Instead of an owner being blessed with an adorable posse of pets, it can quickly turn into a case of pets and owner living miserably ever after. Or, in the extreme case, the owner having to make the awful choice as to who stays and who goes. I promise you, if you read on, it will never come to this.

FIGHTING LIKE CATS AND DOGS? IT AIN'T NECESSARILY SO!

Some of us die-hard pet lovers want the best of both worlds. We want a dog in our lives, but we also want a cat in our home, maybe even a bird or some fish for good measure. Unfortunately, combining these critters under one roof conjures up visions of dogs making hors d'oeuvres out of fuzzy little kitties, Kitty scratching out Fido's eyes, Fido stalking your feathered friend, or even Fido fishing, complete with his own rod and reel, seated in front of the fish tank.

I swear to you, it doesn't have to be that way. Tige and his kitty comrade Mowdy are living proof of this. My dog Tige had been an "only child" in our downstate residence for six years when Mowdy came into the picture. At three years of age, Mowdy was no spring tomcat either when he made the transition from outdoor stray to Tige's indoor housemate. Now I find them sleeping nose to nose on my bed. In fact, on the rare occasion that Mowdy has an overnight stay at the vet, Tige isn't quite his old self—he obviously misses his feline friend. So take heart. When properly introduced, dogs living together under one roof can learn to be best friends, and so can dogs and cats, dogs and birds, dogs and fish, even dogs and mice. It's simply a matter of negotiating their differences and desensitizing the offending pet to its housemate. The steps given below, while designed to encourage dogs to get along, can be applied to all the various pets you want Fido to learn to love.

THE GREAT BIG BOO-BOO

Pet owners make their biggest mistake by just plunking down the new pet into Fido's space. In fact, any instant addition to the family, whether animal or human, may be enough to upset the balance in a dog's life. To gain a better perspective, give some thought as to how you would feel if someone suddenly moved into your home on a long-term basis. Life would become abruptly different: schedules would change, the food in the refrigerator would start to reflect someone else's tastes, and privacy within your own home just wouldn't be what it used to be. Any newly married couple can attest to the changes brought on by cohabitation. Newlyweds, however, are presumably mature adult human beings who are capable of rationalizing those differences, who should be prepared to cope with the stress that might surface when dealing with personality conflicts brought about by married life. Unfortunately, as demonstrated by the high rate of divorce, adult humans don't do very well living together under one roof—so why should we assume that man's best friends will be miraculously different?

I believe there are many similarities between child psychology and pet psychology. Think about it. Young children and pets are both sensitive emotionally. Both have not yet figured out the complexities of our world. In their naïveté they tend to see things differently from adults. That's why I believe a situation I experienced as a child allows me to closely identify with the way pets feel when their space is infringed upon.

When I was little, both my aunt and uncle died, leaving their two young children orphaned. One of those children, a girl about my age, came to live with my family. In retrospect, she was a lovely little girl suffering her own pain and sense of confusion at having lost her parents at a very young age. But at the time I was terribly upset, and jealous of this new kid that had suddenly landed in my home, usurping attention and affection from my parents that I thought should have been reserved just for my sister and me.

Of course, I realize now that I was just too young to really understand what my cousin was going through. At the time, because of all of the attention she received and because I felt pushed aside, there was just no way I was going to like her. Having lived through this experience, I understand the range of emotions that one animal feels when a second animal is suddenly thrown into the picture.

Many of us have come to understand the basic principle I have outlined above. For some of you, it's through your adult experiences with friends, bosses, new babies, and other new family members (just think of all those mother-in-law jokes). Any two or more animals, whether human, canine, feline, or whatever, spending any great amount of time together are bound to run into problems and differences in opinion. The final result depends on the way things are approached.

NEUTRAL TURF

The phrase "neutral turf" is familiar to any teenage gang member. Because neither gang is in charge of a specified territory and since none of the members lives in the neutral zone, there's no need to be protective of the area. It's perceived as a safe place for them to conduct their hooligan business with one another. If, on the other hand, one gang shows up unannounced in the other's territory, the odds are good that there will be fighting, and possibly bloodshed. The group whose neighborhood is invaded feels threatened and perceives a real need to protect themselves, their homes, and their loved ones.

Yes, I know this scenario is beginning to sound a lot like the movie *West Side Story*, but it's true—males do challenge one another for superiority. Although it's not always an exclusively male problem, I have found that the odds of females presenting the same challenge are much less. So for the purposes of this chapter, we'll focus on Fido.

A perfectly happy, well-adjusted dog living comfortably in his perfectly normal home may feel a lot like one of those gang members when another dog arrives unannounced on the scene. *Wham!* With no preparation at all, this perfectly happy, well-adjusted dog has the rug pulled out right from underneath him. It happens all at once, without the slightest early warning signal.

Keeping this in mind, you can substantially reduce the risk of trouble if you introduce your dogs to each other on neutral turf. If possible, arrange to bring Fido to a friend's home so he can meet his future housemate. Let them check each other out for a few minutes, then take Fido home alone. Follow up this meeting with several play sessions on neutral territory, always taking Fido home alone. When the dogs seem to really be enjoying each other's company, make arrangements for the big day when the new dog comes home with his "old buddy." Voilà, everyone's in one home and happy to be there.

I know a lot of you are shaking your heads and saying, "Is this guy kidding? That's an awful lot of time and effort to go through." Well, you'll get no argument from me that this does take a bit of effort on your part, but I can assure you it takes a whole lot less time than dealing with an aggression problem later on. An ounce of prevention goes a long, long way.

SEPARATE BUT EQUAL TIME

It's only natural that family members and visitors will want to coo over the new dog (especially if he's a puppy) once he comes home, but try not to do that in front of your other dog. Save such special attention for private times, setting aside a few five-minute sessions each day alone with each pet. Prevent jealousy by having somebody take one of the pets elsewhere before you do all the private smooching. If that can't be arranged, put the other pet in a large closed-off room with all sorts of extraordinary special treats and goodies to help occupy him. Be sure to turn up the volume of a TV or radio in that room to help drown out your cooing over the new pet.

IT'S PARTY TIME

Make it seem that wonderful things happen to dog number one whenever dog number two is on the scene. Exaggerate everything so that this new lifestyle, including a new housemate, seems to be the best thing that's ever happened to dog number one. Remember to include the extra goodies, treats, hugs, and kisses. Every time dog number one is around dog number two, there should be such a wonderful fuss that he thinks you're throwing a party just for him. If roast beef is his favorite thing in the world, give him some when the other dog is around. Make him feel like he's just won the million-dollar lottery. I call this party-time association. Dogs learn by association, and if they associate their togetherness with such fabulous fringe benefits, it will help them to realize that life's been a blast ever since they met. In this way pet number one will never see pet number two as an intruder. Instead, they will begin to see each other as catalysts for a good time.

Next, be sure there are plenty of toys and bones so that neither dog becomes possessive over playthings. You say each one of your pets has five or six toys. What a sport you are! In my book, plenty of playthings means dozens. Forcing dogs to vie over a few precious toys and bones is bound to bring out their worst sides; it's a perfect way to create aggression. Additionally, too few toys may encourage one dog to bother another out of sheer boredom.

During the honeymoon period, when the dogs are first getting to know one another, there should be so many toys scattered all over the place that, if you get up in the middle of the night and don't almost kill yourself on all the stuff on the floor, you're lucky. Seriously, there should be all sorts of things thrown about to occupy the dogs' attention at any given moment. A dog that's thinking of being feisty or rowdy (or worse, nasty) isn't going to wander down the hallway, past the bedroom, through the kitchen, and into the den to get to his toys. He's more likely to annoy the other dog, especially if he's nearby. But if there are all sorts of goodies around waiting to distract Fido, the chances of a fight are greatly diminished.

During the "getting to know you" stage, frequently change all the play items you've bought for them. It will help keep things interesting. I suggest you add, subtract, and rotate as many toys and bones as your wallet allows.

THE CHARLES BRONSON SYNDROME

Some dogs develop what I call the Charles Bronson syndrome. You know the type. A bully. He's the dog who, if he had his choice, would be wearing a black leather jacket and sporting a tattoo. This dog decides, in no uncertain terms, that no other dog is going to live in his space under any circumstances, period, the end. This is the dog with whom you must negotiate and be prepared to take things step-by-step.

The first point to consider is that this dog can't—or won't—tolerate anything about a new canine companion. You'll need to begin with one little piece of the puzzle at a time. Record a friend's talkative dog or buy a sound effects record containing dog barks and whines. Play the recording at a very low volume for a few days or weeks until Fido shows no reaction. Then increase the volume for a few more days or weeks until the dog seems unperturbed by it. Continue the process until the recording is playing at full blast and Charles Bronson doesn't seem to mind.

The next step is bring home a few items that carry the odor of the new dog. Towels or pet bedding are ideal. Leave them around the house for Fido to find. Replace them every few days with new items that have a stronger, fresh scent. During this process, apply the "party time" advice I gave on page 74. This will allow your tough guy to slowly get used to the smells and the sounds he views as competitive, without becoming overwhelmed by the real thing. If you're concerned that Fido may become really vicious, introduce a stuffed animal that resembles a real dog as much as possible and that has actually been around a real dog so that it has picked up its scent. Play the taped barks at the same time. By creating conditions that simulate a dog before the new dog's arrival, the risk factor of serious fighting later will be substantially reduced.

As described earlier, the dogs should be introduced on neutral turf. Later, just before you bring the new dog home, install a very tall pet gate, or place one gate on top of another, high enough so that neither dog can jump over it. Since we anticipate hostility, the gate will prevent tough-guy Fido from terrorizing the other dog. Let them live on opposite sides of the gate for a while. Allow them to see and sniff each other while you continue using all the steps for first-dog psychology previously described. Don't worry if at first they growl, snarl, and compete for your attention. The four-legged canine kids may behave just like jealous two-legged human kids. But gradually, and it might be very slowly, that game will get old and they'll start to forget about each other.

When things seem safe, and behavior around the gate has been calm for a few weeks, take it down for a little while each day. Be sure each dog is securely restrained by a collar and leash. More than likely you'll need a friend or family member for this step. By controlling the dogs on leashes, you'll allow them more freedom and also simulate a more normal household environment without allowing them so much freedom that they run amok. The bad news is that all the snarling and growling that ended weeks ago may begin again as you embark on this step of the process. In fact, it may seem a bit like in Monopoly when you get the card that says "Go directly to jail. Do not pass go." Yes, I know it's a bit depressing, but don't get discouraged. Know that the snarling and growling will run its course and slowly disappear. Be patient and remember that whenever you're dealing with a serious dog problem, it's normal to experience ups and downs on the progress scale. Be reassured that the dogs are behaving in the expected manner.

STAY CALM AND DON'T JUMP IN TOO FAST

When our pets are learning to adjust to each other it sometimes sounds like a nuclear explosion. When this happens, owners need to be careful not to interfere too quickly. I know the sounds of such a confrontation can be horrendous, but often what looks and sounds so serious is simply your pets getting to know each other. Your interfering can make them feel there is something really intense going on and may actually create the very aggression problem you're looking to avoid.

Just when do you butt in? This is one of the hardest judgment calls for owners to make. If you break things up too early, you run the risk of contributing to the problem. If you wait too long, you may be encouraging a serious fight. Since each dog varies greatly in its personality and temperament, there's no easy answer. Try to be very observant of each dog's body language: the position of the ears, dilation of the pupils, the position of the tail (see pages 21–24). Let things go as long as you can, but separate the dogs before any of these signs become overly exaggerated. Of course, when in doubt, don't take chances. It's better to break things up too soon than make a mistake and have a fight take place.

PATIENCE IS A DOG EDUCATOR'S VIRTUE

I'm always amazed when people contact me and say they've tried everything I've suggested and had no results. When I ask how long they've been following my advice, I inevitably hear answers in terms of weeks. It may have been two or three weeks before they threw in the proverbial towel. I then ask them how long and how many tries it took them to quit smoking or shed those extra pounds. I know I failed miserably on both counts several times before I finally prevailed. It's a rare individual who can say they succeeded on the first try. The point is that it can take time to break bad habits.

While it's true that many of my clients experience immediate (or nearly immediate) results with many of their pets' problems, and while this makes me look like the greatest dog expert that ever walked the face of the earth, the truth is you should consider yourself very lucky if things fall into place right away. It's only reasonable to assume that behavior, particularly habits that have been ingrained in a dog's personality over months or years, may take some time to change. Yes, you can teach an old dog new tricks—you just have to have patience and perseverance. How long will it take? That's difficult to say. After all, so much is determined by the individual dog and what his personal experiences have been. This can be an especially big challenge with dogs adopted from shelters or taken in as strays—you may have no clues to their past experiences. Think of it as therapy. How long does it take someone to resolve deep-rooted psychological problems? Some people do quite well, making dramatic improvements quickly. Others need a therapy support system for years. Fortunately, dogs rarely take that long. Nonetheless, many owners tend to be impatient, often giving up just before a major breakthrough.

Aggressive, nasty behavior may take the longest of any problem to rectify. Keep at it and you'll more than likely be pleased with the results. Feisty, fighting canines may never become bosom buddies, but there's a 90 percent chance they'll at least learn to tolerate each other and maintain some form of household harmony.

Finally, if you follow the steps I've outlined, don't be surprised if something magical happens. One day, when you least expect it, you may walk in and catch your pets snoozing together, nose-to-nose, cuddled up ever so close—friends for life.

WHAT TO EXPECT FROM FIDO WHEN YOU'RE EXPECTING

THE QUESTION MOST COMMONLY ASKED BY PARENTS- AND GRANDPARENTS-TO-BE

I can't tell you how many hundreds of times I've been asked the following question by worried parents- and grandparents-to-be: "Warren, we're expecting our first child (or grandchild) and we don't know how Fido is going to react."

Scared by horror stories, told by well-meaning but ill-informed relatives and friends, of dogs snapping at babies and cats smothering sleeping infants, couples expecting their first child often resort to giving away their pets or, even worse, having them destroyed.

WHY IS THIS SIBLING RIVALRY SCENARIO SO PREVALENT?

With the advent of two-income families and the trend toward postponing childbearing in favor of career advancement, very often Fido is a couple's first "baby." Any pet preexisting the birth of a child could be subject to jealousy or aggression created by fear, confusion, or even protective feelings for the mother. After all, he probably had first place in the hearts of the couple, receiving an inordinate amount of attention, including birthday presents, special time at the park, even "grandparents" that called him their grandpuppy. Having all this stripped away when the real baby arrives can create major problems, but it doesn't have to be this way.

THE BIGGEST MISTAKE— NOT PLANNING AHEAD

All too often people ask for my advice on this situation *after* the baby has arrived. Generally I hear, "We've got a new baby at home and we're afraid to let Fido near the baby."

Shame on you! Mother Nature generally gives you an eight- or nine-month period of time to prepare for your baby's arrival. This is ample time to prepare Fido for your family's newest addition, too.

MY SEVEN EASY STEPS TO EASE THE NEW ARRIVAL

STEP ONE: DESENSITIZE FIDO TO THE SIGHTS, SOUNDS, AND SMELLS OF A NEW BABY

Be sure Fido feels comfortable with all the sights, sounds, and odors that are part and parcel of a new baby several months prior to the baby's arrival. Do this by introducing Fido to mobiles and rattles, and to the sound of a crying baby, by recording the cries of a friend's infant or purchasing a sound effects record. Play it at a low volume, and give Fido lots of positive attention while it's playing. Do this for a few minutes each day. Every few days, when he displays no reaction to it, gradually increase the volume.

Place baby powder, baby oil, and diapers on the floor and allow Fido to sniff around them. Also, mix a little ammonia with water and place it on the diaper, simulating the odor of a dirty diaper. This will help fend off housebreaking regressions when Fido, sensing that the baby is allowed to have accidents, thinks, "If it's okay for the baby, then it must be okay for me."

STEP TWO: IT'S TIME TO PLAY HOUSE

You may label me eccentric after I describe the next important step (and heaven forbid I be labeled eccentric!). Go out and purchase a doll that resembles a newborn, and play house. That's right! The two of you should hold, cuddle, and coo over the doll as if it were the real McCoy! Granted, you may not want the neighbors or your in-laws to see you doing this, but there is definitely a reason for doing so. Many dogs become jealous when Mom's being affectionate with a baby, and they're then commanded to move away or are sent outdoors. By beginning with the doll, you'll work out all the kinks and won't be as fearful of Fido hurting the baby.

STEP THREE: IT'S TIME FOR A
TRIP TO THE VET

Be sure that Fido has a physical exam prior to the new baby's arrival. You'll have the peace of mind of knowing that he is free of parasites such as worms and fleas, is up-to-date on all his vaccinations, and has had his nails trimmed to avoid accidental scratches.

STEP FOUR: WHEN MOM'S GONE
TO THE HOSPITAL

While their wives are hospitalized, new fathers are frantically juggling time spent on the job, at the hospital, caring for the home, and keeping Fido on schedule. Something has got to give, and usually it's Fido's routine. Have a neighbor with whom Fido is familiar stand by to take over. There's nothing worse for a dog than going through the upheaval of missed meals, fewer and shorter walks, and loneliness and then coping with a newborn's arrival.

STEP FIVE: WHEN MOM RETURNS HOME

When it's time for Mom to come home, she should walk in alone, without the baby. (Have Dad stay in the car with the newborn.) Fido will be excited to see Mom, and this special time alone will allow Mom to give (and receive) the big greeting. If Mom was holding the baby, her natural reaction might be to pull away, fearful that Fido's crazy antics might hurt the infant, and thus setting the stage for jealousy. Once the reunion is completed, Dad may enter with the newest addition to the family.

STEP SIX: WHEN GUESTS VISIT
THE NEW BABY

Be sure there is a stack of new doggy toys on hand when family and friends come to visit the new baby. Upon each visitor's arrival, have them hand Fido a new toy and insist that they greet and coo over Fido as if he were the center of attention before they go in to see the new baby. Remember, we want Fido to think that the arrival of the new baby is the best thing that's ever happened to him! Never let Fido feel he's being left out of the excitement.

STEP SEVEN: COMMON SENSE DICTATES NEVER LEAVE A BABY ALONE WITH A PET

No matter how well you and Fido have progressed through the previous six steps, *never* leave an infant or young child alone with a pet. After all, despite all the precautions you can take, accidents still do happen. It would be irresponsible to leave any baby or young child unattended—regardless of whether there's a pet in the household. And while Fido may be a great companion for your child, don't assume he's a four-footed baby-sitter!

BABY AND FIDO—FRIENDS FOR LIFE

By putting a little time and effort in before baby's arrival, there's no reason why Fido and your child can't be friends for life! And remember, numerous studies now indicate that kids that grow up with pets are generally better adjusted than those who do not.

SEX AND THE
SINGLE DOG

The rendezvous was arranged. All the romantic details were in place. He was dark and handsome and eager. She waited in anticipation, her golden hair shimmering in the sunlight. They were both shy and inexperienced. She stood nervously, unable to look at him. She wanted to stare deeply into his large, soulful eyes, but she couldn't bring herself to do it. All she could do was stare at her feet, all four of them.

She and he were pedigreed poodles, brought together for a union that would hopefully bear the fruits of their loving experience, a litter of adorable puppies. But when the big day arrived, neither dog knew what to do; they were willing but didn't have a clue.

Questions about your pets' sexuality don't end with wanting to know about breeding pedigreed dogs. Owners have loads of questions about their pets' sexuality, but they're afraid to ask. Now you don't have to—the answers are here.

THE BEST SEX
IS NO SEX

The most important rule for sex and the single dog is that there should be no sex. There is a massive overpopulation problem resulting in the killing of millions of healthy pets each year—for no other reason than a lack of homes. According to conservative estimates, in just seven years one dog and her offspring can produce thousands of puppies. Multiply that by a few extra years and the numbers boggle the mind. I've cried more than a few tears and saved more than a few dogs from the shelters' death chambers. If you've ever walked the halls of an animal shelter and seen all those little paws reaching out from behind their prison bars, just begging for a little human contact, you'll understand my concern. If you've never had the experience, try it. I guarantee it will break your heart, but it may encourage your help in solving the problems that have created the mass murder that takes place with unwanted dogs.

Realize, however, that no one individual or group of individuals can drastically reduce those numbers by rescue and adoption alone. The only solution is the prevention of reproduction in the first place. In other words, the best sex is no sex.

THE ULTIMATE FORM OF BIRTH
CONTROL—
SPAYING AND NEUTERING

Any dog that might get together with dogs of the opposite sex should be neutered or spayed. The only exception should be pedigreed dogs that are extraordinary representatives of their breeds. My feelings on this subject run deep and strong. The massive killing of healthy, homeless pets each year has gotten out of hand. As far as I'm concerned, indiscriminate breeding is a cardinal sin.

Neutering is the term generally used for altering, or castrating, males. Spaying, a type of hysterectomy, is the term used for females. In addition to removing the ability to breed, spaying and neutering are considered by some animal health professionals as a means to lessen the incidence of cancer of the reproductive system. A lesser known alternative, one that is not widely practiced but is available, is vasectomies for males. This procedure sterilizes them but leaves them physically and sexually intact.

WILL FIXING FIDO CREATE BETTER BEHAVIOR?

Neutering and spaying are often suggested as a means of resolving pet behavioral problems and calming a hyperactive personality. However, I don't always agree. Neutering and spaying are not magic wands for dealing with behavior problems! Dogs should be neutered and spayed for reasons of health and birth control. Behavioral problems, particularly when they've developed into well-established habits, should be dealt with by a training and behavioral therapy program. For instance, a male dog's indiscriminate urinating, once begun, may not be helped by neutering alone.

MISCONCEPTIONS ABOUT SPAYING AND NEUTERING

The big misconception is that dogs, once they're spayed or neutered, become fat and lazy. Only those dogs whose owners have a heavy hand on the can opener, providing too much food and too little exercise, will become grossly out of shape. This holds true whether or not the dog has been spayed or neutered.

Spaying and neutering will not negatively affect the looks and personality of your pet. Once a gorgeous dog, always a gorgeous dog.

Despite what you may have heard, a female does not need to be bred at least once. And, finally, it is not a good idea to allow her to have one litter in order for your children to witness the miracle of birth.

WHEN'S THE BIG DAY?

Veterinarians differ on exactly what age dogs should be spayed or neutered, but most agree that it should be done within the first year. There's even a growing trend toward neutering and spaying at very early ages—as early as eight weeks old. However, if your dog is older, the operation can certainly still be performed, providing Fido is healthy enough for surgery. Simply check with your vet.

BIRTH CONTROL ALTERNATIVES

If you have personal reasons for not spaying or neutering your dog, then adhere to the next best form of birth control—a leash. No unaltered dog should be permitted to run free—you'll just be contributing to the tragic overpopulation problem. You should also, of course, keep Fluffy away from dogs of the opposite sex that live in your home. There are products available through veterinarians that can help delay a heat cycle, but they're generally recommended for short-term use only—not for birth control.

OOPS! WHAT ARE THOSE SIX TINY THINGS CUDDLED UP IN THE BACK OF THE CLOSET?

Should an unwanted pregnancy occur, a veterinarian can terminate it in its early stages. If personal beliefs prevent you from having the pregnancy terminated or, if by some mystery, there's a litter of puppies you didn't know anything about, you should be responsible for that litter. And that doesn't mean dumping the tiny puppies off at the local overcrowded and underfunded humane society. The litter is your responsibility. Care for them. Then locate good, loving homes for each defenseless puppy. Finally, get that dog spayed!

IF YOU'RE DEAD SET ON BREEDING . . .

Only dogs of exceptional pedigree quality, falling well within the written standards for that breed as outlined by the American Kennel Club and deemed excellent by a professional dog-show judge, should be considered for breeding purposes. The national breed club branch in your area, whose listing is available through the AKC, may help you to locate a good mate, but generally only owners of proven champions will be encouraged to breed their dogs.

Pets should be fully mature before breeding. Opinions vary as to when a pet is mature. I personally think it is at two years of age, and sometimes more. Many dogs who are younger than that are either physically or emotionally juvenile, neither of which is the best criterion for good parenting.

One of the two partners should be experienced. Although two amateurs may be interested in each other, they may not be able to figure out exactly what they need to do. In that case, it's up to the owners to literally get in the act, helping demonstrate all the right moves. Aren't you thrilled? I bet you didn't know that being responsible for Fido's or Fluffy's sexual instruction—being a kind of canine Mrs. Robinson or Casanova—was part of your job description as an owner!

If all goes well between Fido and Fluffy, Fluffy's appetite will increase and so will the size of her belly. Approximately sixty-three days later there should be a litter of highly adorable puppies.

CAN FIDO BE A HOMOSEXUAL?

This is a very popular question, and the answer isn't what people expect. Many types of animals exhibit homosexual tendencies while still having a heterosexual preference. Some experts think man is one of the few animals that suppresses these tendencies. While it's true dogs will occasionally show an interest in dogs of the same sex, very often they're simply demonstrating dominant behavior as a form of power play. It's usually not sexually related.

MOUNTING, OR WHAT'S LESS TASTEFULLY CALLED HUMPING

One of the most embarrassing moments for any dog owner is when Fido mounts a visitor in your home.

My all-time favorite mounting story involves two former clients of mine, comedian Rodney Dangerfield and his dog Keno. I was called in to resolve a housebreaking problem that had Rodney's dog relieving himself all over the comedian's New

York City apartment. It had gotten to the point where Keno's puddles had actually shorted out his owner's elaborate and expensive exercise bicycle. While I was there I had the luxury of hearing a Dangerfield classic. He confided to me that a mounting problem was also taking place. In his inimitable style he said, "Talk about no respect—my dog closes his eyes before he mounts my leg."

Mounting, also referred to as humping, takes place when a pet physically attaches itself to an item carrying a strong human odor, often a pillow or bathrobe; jumps sexually on another pet; or becomes attached to someone's leg. That leg usually belongs to a guest you're trying to impress—like your boss or a new date. It seems that our pets have an uncanny knack for humiliating their owners!

Although mounting is sometimes a sexual response, it very often has more to do with dominant behavior than anything sexual; it's simply a display of who's the boss. We human animals view it strictly in sexual terms, but the animal kingdom sees it in terms of power and control. That's why mounting may be demonstrated by both males and females.

If mounting is a constant problem with your dog, more frequent exercise sessions, more mental stimulation, and the teaching of basic commands such as "no" will help keep this behavior in check. Constant mounting may also be a red flag that you're misguiding Fido in your day-to-day teaching approach.

Can mounting be helped by neutering or spaying? Sometimes yes and sometimes no, but never count on surgery to correct possible behavior problems. As I indicated earlier, the primary purpose for neutering and spaying is birth control, not behavior control.

CAN FLUFFY BE A NYMPHOMANIAC?

I know you're thinking, "This sounds like the topic of a bad TV talk show trying to get good ratings." Nevertheless, Fluffy can be a nymphomaniac due to excessive hormone production in her body (hyperestrinism is the medical term). A similar problem can also occur in males (satyriasis). These males and females can experience an increased interest in riding or mounting anything. Your best friend may also develop a Jekyll and Hyde personality—becoming aggressive at peak times. Veterinarians can usually treat this problem, and neutering or spaying is often recommended.

FALSE PREGNANCY

The old saying "There's no such thing as being a little bit pregnant" doesn't quite hold true for some pets. There is a "sort of" pregnancy that can occur at any time, even when no male dog is involved—the false pregnancy. While usually brought on by a hormonal imbalance, I've seen a few that were purely psychological.

False pregnancies are just that—false. Fluffy's not actually pregnant but shows many of the medical or emotional signs that she might be. In its mildest form, a dog will "nest" with some of her favorite toys or her owner's personal belongings, treating these items like puppies. An owner's fuzzy slippers or cuddly, soft sweaters or the kids' stuffed animals might disappear, only to turn up piled in a corner behind a chair. Quite often these items will be wet and yucky from the confused mama dog licking and nurturing them. When it's more serious, there are physical signs, including swelling of the abdomen. Some vets let the mild form simply run its course with no real intervention. With more serious cases, medications and spaying are sometimes the suggested solutions. In strictly psychological cases, I've seen dogs exhibit signs of false pregnancy even after spaying. Experience has taught me that when it comes to dealing with behavior, anything is possible.

ONE FINAL PIECE OF ADVICE

Don't shy away from asking your vet questions about your dog's sexuality—there's nothing to be afraid of. And understanding it will make Fluffy's and Fido's lives happier and healthier.

CANINE KINDERGARTEN

GET A HEAD START ON FIDO'S EDUCATION

As soon as Fido comes into your life, he's ready for the at-home version of Canine Kindergarten. Make it fun, and don't overly structure anything. Guide him gently in the right direction. Don't overuse corrections—give him lots of praise and love instead.

When I say start Fido's education early, I mean early—as early as eight weeks old. Some people will certainly argue with me on this point. Many experts suggest waiting until Fido's older, but I believe that when he's old enough to get into the garbage, he's old enough to learn not to get into it. When Rambo Fido is old enough to hold the cat hostage, he's old enough to learn how to be friends instead. In other words, let's take that same energy and intelligence Fido uses to cause trouble and channel it into positive, desirable behavior.

I wish I had a nickel for every call I've ever received from owners at their wits' end due to their puppies' misbehavior. I'd be a very wealthy man! Calls such as "Fido chewed the new sofa to shreds," "Fluffy jumps up on everyone who comes into the house," "Fido's eaten my Gucci shoes," or "Fluffy does her business on the new carpet." (By the way, when I hear that phrase, I picture Fluffy walking down the hall with a little briefcase!) Inevitably I discover that Fluffy and Fido are four, five, even six months old and these problems have been going on for months.

What a waste! All those weeks and months of negative behavior could have been avoided, or at least nipped in the bud, had Fido and Fluffy started Canine Kindergarten early. In fact, the longer the negative behavior has been going on, the longer it will take to undo that behavior. I've actually worked with dogs who answered to the name No because they were constantly being corrected by their owners for their bad behavior! It's important to remember, however, that it's never too late to channel that negative energy into positive behavior. In other words, while it's best to start young, you *can* teach an old dog new tricks!

And I can't blame Fido's and Fluffy's owners for getting a late start on their pets' educations. A lot of obedience schools won't accept puppy pupils until they reach six months of age. If these so-called professionals won't train our pets until they reach a certain age, how can the average owner think he or she can? Having worked with over forty thousand different animals, with the majority of them being puppies, I say you can and should start Fido's education early.

In addition to untorn sofas, uneaten Gucci shoes and spot-free carpets, there's an additional benefit to Fido's early education. The earlier he's introduced to things in a fun way, the less traumatic it will be for him to learn later on. This type of early training develops a certain self-confidence in our pets.

The only exception to this early education program involves excursions to the great outdoors. Check with the vet to determine when Fido's vaccinations will give him enough protection to go outside.

Think of basic training as the doggy alphabet. Teaching Fido his behavioral ABCs will give you a positive way to communicate with your four-footed best friend.

LESSON NUMBER ONE: POTTY ETIQUETTE

TO HOUSEBREAK OR TO PAPER-TRAIN— A DECISION TO MAKE BEFORE FIDO'S ARRIVAL

Like every owner, you are confronted with one of two choices if you want to keep your home from smelling like a kennel: housebreaking or paper-training. There are very distinct reasons for choosing one approach over the other. Make the wrong decision in the beginning and the results can be disastrous. Potty etiquette or the lack of potty etiquette can be the undermining factor in many a dog-owner relationship. Failure to teach Fido to urinate and defecate where you want him to is perhaps the single most common reason for Fido winding up in the local animal shelter. It doesn't have to happen.

So plan ahead what you want Fido to do and where you want him to do it. Don't take a hit-and-miss attitude, then blame him when he does a "hit-and-miss" on your carpet. By giving a little advance thought to the situation, Fido can be very easily housebroken or paper-trained. Yes, you can have a puppy and walk barefoot in the house!

PAPER-TRAINING—A MISNOMER

When you hear the term "paper-training," you generally think of Fido eliminating—going potty, doing his business, pooping, or peeing—on a few sheets of *The Wall Street Journal* or your local newspaper. In reality, you should not use your daily newspaper in this process, as the newsprint gets on Fido's paws, resulting in tiny black paw prints all over your home. Fido may even lick his paws and ingest the ink. Instead, I recommend using absorbent pads made especially for this purpose. These so-called wee-wee pads are safer for our pets and feature the additional benefit of absorbing the urine, thereby eliminating some of the odor. Another alternative is to use unprinted newspaper, which can often be obtained free of charge at newspaper printing plants.

So for simplicity's sake, I will use the term "paper-training" to mean the use of these specially made pads or unprinted newspaper, not your daily newspaper. Now that we've got our definitions straight, there's a decision to be made.

TO HOUSEBREAK OR NOT TO HOUSEBREAK— THAT IS THE QUESTION

With very few exceptions (see the following section), Fido should always be housebroken.

WHEN PAPER-TRAINING IS CALLED FOR

Some circumstances dictate that a dog be totally paper-trained. For instance, an apartment dweller may find life much easier when Fido uses the pads or unprinted paper. This avoids the problem of bringing him down several flights of stairs or the risk of him having an accident in the elevator just when the superintendent happens to appear. Also, if the old neighborhood ain't what it used to be, you might not want to be walking Fido late at night. This is an exceptionally popular option for women and older folks living in urban areas, especially if Fido would hardly scare off a criminal. And yes, there is a convenience factor to paper-training Fido. He doesn't have to be walked in the rain, snow, heat, and cold, or when you're home sick in bed. If you're one of those people who works incredibly long hours, you'll have the peace of mind of knowing that Fido isn't sitting with his little doggy legs crossed waiting for you to come home to walk him.

Some vets will recommend you keep your puppy indoors until he has completed his vaccinations, particularly if you live in an urban area without the luxury of a private yard. In this instance, paper-training is your best option. The same applies for working families who are away from home eight to ten hours a day. It is neither physically possible nor healthy for a young puppy to "hold" for this length of time.

THE BIG HOUSEBREAKING BOO-BOO

Unless you have a definite reason for paper-training Fido, housebreak him immediately and directly. Directly means without using paper-training as an intermediate step. This is one of the biggest mistakes new dog owners make.

Let's look at it from Fido's point of view. By paper-training Fido, you're telling him to urinate and defecate in the house on pads or paper. Then you're reprimanding him for urinating and defecating in the house off the pads or paper. Then you're asking him to relieve himself outside without pads or paper. By first telling him it's good to go in the house, then it's bad to go in the house, you're potentially creating a neurotic situation. Boy, I'd sure be confused!

The intermediate step of paper-training during the housebreaking process is enough to drive Fido crazy, and ultimately he'll drive you crazy, too. After all, this step breaks the consistency necessary for any form of successful training. So if your vet says it's okay for Fido to go out before his series of vaccinations are completed—this is most likely to occur if your live in a suburban area with a private yard exclusively for Fido's use—go directly to the housebreaking steps in the next sections.

THE KEY TO SUCCESSFUL HOUSEBREAKING— PATIENCE, NOT PANIC

Housebreaking is not that difficult if you take a methodical, step-by-step approach. You'll be surprised how capable young puppies are of "holding" themselves. Unfortunately, too many owners panic when faced with a housebreaking problem and enlist the aid and suggestions of various well-meaning friends and family members. Sadly, much of the advice given is incorrect and, at times, even inhumane. How many times have you heard someone proudly proclaim, "If my dog pees in the house, I just stick his nose in it." Would you do that to your own child when you're potty-training him? Of course you wouldn't!

Finally, your friend's method of housebreaking may have worked for his dog, but that doesn't guarantee that it will work for yours. Some dogs, regardless of what method is used, will learn and become housebroken. Owners of these dogs are lucky. But it takes patience and a thorough understanding of every step in the housebreaking process to housebreak many dogs. Most important—do not panic.

The following steps have proven successful with tens of thousands of dogs. This approach does not teach Fido to go outside per se, but does teach him that never, under any circumstances, is he allowed to go inside. Therefore, his natural conclusion is to go outdoors. This approach tries to avoid a situation in which he urinates and defecates both outdoors and inside.

CONFINEMENT

Anytime Fido cannot be supervised or watched closely, he should be confined. Begin by gating off a small area of a room in your home with one of those adjustable puppy gates. I find the kitchen to be ideal for this, since linoleum or tile floors make cleanup so much easier. When Fido remains clean in that small area for two days, gradually increase the size of the area.

CONFINEMENT—A STEP IN THE HOUSEBREAKING PROCESS, NOT A PUPPY-SITTING DEVICE

Unfortunately, some busy owners get in the habit of leaving Fido confined at all times—even when they are home and could be supervising him. They state that they are simply too busy to watch the dog. If you anticipate doing this after you bring your newest family member home, you should think twice about getting a puppy in the first place. Maybe a fish is better suited for your lifestyle!

Confining Fido all the time is very bad for him and is bound to create even more problems later on.

CONFINEMENT—A NECESSARY STEP IN SUCCESSFUL HOUSEBREAKING

Other owners go to the opposite extreme and feel that Fido should not be confined at all. They should realize that confinement is the quickest, easiest, and most efficient way to teach housebreaking. My years of experience working with all types of dogs has convinced me that it's better for Fido if he is quickly taught what to do—then everyone, including his owners, can stop worrying about it. By dragging out the process, both you and Fido will be unhappy and neurotic.

REGULATING FIDO'S SYSTEM

To housebreak Fido quickly and efficiently, it's important to regulate his system. If you can get him to urinate and defecate at the same time every day, you will know when to get him outside and can prevent many an accident from occurring.

WHAT GOES IN MUST COME OUT

Unfortunately, Fido doesn't come equipped with a little dial with which to regulate his system. Instead, it's necessary for you to have him on a diet conducive to housebreaking.

A diet that is overly abundant in meat may be too rich for some of our young four-footed best friends, causing loose and/or frequent bowel movements and flatulence. (Okay, okay—gas!) Foods that need water added to them sometimes will pass through Fido's system too rapidly, causing additional problems and discomfort. Some of the convenience foods, often those packaged in clear cellophane, have a tendency to increase Fido's thirst. The result—he drinks more water than usual, causing more of a problem in housebreaking. Don't get me wrong. By all means Fido should be given a sufficient amount of water, but since some foods make him less thirsty, take advantage of this fact.

A diet of table scraps and other human foods should be avoided in general and especially during housebreaking. Such a diet not only raises questions concerning nutrition during this formative period of Fido's life, it will also not aid in the regulation of his system. After all, human foods and table scraps vary from day to day. Each time Fido eats a different type of food, a different amount of time is required for that food to be digested. Once you have chosen a diet for the housebreaking period—consult with your vet if you're having trouble deciding which to choose—stick with it. The idea is not to upset Fido's regulation by feeding him different diets on different days.

REGULATING FIDO'S WATER INTAKE DURING THE HOUSEBREAKING PERIOD

Although it is important that Fido receive sufficient water, remember that free access to it during his housebreaking period can create a flood of problems. (Sorry, I couldn't resist the metaphor!)

Many professionals in the dog industry will disagree with me, emphatically stating that all dogs, especially puppies, must have free access to water. Their intentions are good. They want to guarantee that the novice owner does not physically harm his dog by failing to provide sufficient water. However, if you continually leave water out for Fido, he may drink a little now and then, and then urinate in the same manner. With this approach, you will never be able to anticipate Fido's needs.

To determine how much water Fido should receive each day, you'll have to consider his weight, age, breed, normal activity level, and the climate he's living in. It's best to consult with your vet. Once you've determined what his daily water intake should be, set up a controlled schedule for giving him water. If you're home during the day, set up your schedule accordingly, giving only a small amount of water at eight P.M., and nothing after that time. If you're gone during the day, then you will have to adjust Fido's water supply accordingly. Here, again, check with your vet.

SCHEDULING FIDO AND YOURSELF

Regardless of how crazy or hectic your own lifestyle might be, Fido is very adaptable and will ultimately adjust to your hours. During the housebreaking period, however, sticking to a proper walking schedule is a must—especially if Fido is a young puppy.

THERE IS SUCH A THING AS TOO MANY WALKS!

One housebreaking theory contends that during this process the dog must be walked every hour on the hour. Although this method gives Fido more than ample time to relieve himself, it does not really teach him what is expected. A dog that is walked too frequently does not learn how to hold himself. Sometimes he'll even forget why he's going outside! After all, no dog could possibly relieve himself each and every hour on the hour. Too many walks are just as bad as too few walks. From a practical standpoint, in this era of two-income households, only people who are willing to give up their vacations would ever own a housebroken canine!

THE IDEAL SCHEDULE FOR FIDO

In general, the first waking person of the household wins the dubious honor of walking Fido in the morning. If you're that person, I bet you're thrilled! But you might also be the one who must rush off to work and therefore cannot walk him. In this situation you have two options: Either you must awaken earlier to walk Fido, or someone else in the family must get up and do it.

The fact of the matter is that when you wake up, Fido also wakes up. He's been holding for six to ten hours and has to go. You cannot expect him to wait until you have showered, shaved, fed the kids breakfast, or had your first cup of coffee. He must be taken care of immediately. After his walk, you may feed him breakfast at your convenience. However, the immediacy of the feeding is not as crucial as that of the first walk of the day. Fido should be taken out again approximately fifteen minutes after being fed.

Fido's next group of daily walks will vary depending on his age. If he's a very young puppy, he should have walks every two to three hours. Between the ages of six and eight months, walks should be every four to six hours, and when Fido is eight months of age or older, every six to eight hours.

Regardless of Fido's age, he should be walked after dinner during the housebreaking period. This should never be later than six P.M. and preferably should be as early as five P.M. The next walk should be scheduled around seven-thirty or eight P.M. The last walk of the day should be just before your bedtime.

If Fido is a young puppy, count on taking him for additional walks after every nap and after playing. Young puppies go at these times like clockwork!

By now you must be saying, "What have I gotten myself into? That's an awful lot of walks!" Take heart! This type of walking pattern does not continue forever. This is simply for the housebreaking period. As Fido progresses, the number of walks he'll need will decrease as the number of hours between walks increases.

ACCIDENTS WILL HAPPEN

Although Fido's housebreaking might be going along smoothly, all of a sudden he might have an accident. Regardless of who's to blame—maybe you gave him too much water or got him off his schedule—he must be told that this behavior is wrong. And that doesn't mean rubbing his nose in it. Nor does it mean taking him to his accident and saying, "What did you do?" First of all, do you really expect an answer? Second, this corrective approach is merely telling him that he shouldn't go in that spot. And he won't. Instead, he'll go a little to the left or a little to the right or maybe in a totally different room.

The point is that Fido must learn that the act of going anywhere in the house is incorrect. Whenever an accident is found, pick it up (or blot it up using a paper towel), then take Fido and the mess to another area and confine him with it for twenty minutes. You should return every ten minutes and tell Fido "No!" In this way he will learn that no matter where he goes in the house, he will be confined with his mess. He'll catch on amazingly fast!

CLEANING UP THE ACCIDENT

One of the most overlooked components of the housebreaking process is the thorough cleaning of the areas where Fido has had accidents. An improperly cleaned floor is an open invitation for Fido to keep going in the house. The odor tells him, "Gee, this must be the right place." And just because you can't smell the odor doesn't mean that Fido's keen nose can't detect it.

The most common mistake owners make is reaching for a household cleaning product containing ammonia to clean up the mess. Ammonia-based products actually encourage Fido to return to the scene of the crime, because urine, too, contains ammonia. In essence, you're putting the identical odor all over the floor. If you've ever changed a baby's wet diaper, you know exactly what I'm talking about!

Other items commonly used as floor cleaners during the housebreaking process are vinegar and club soda. Since your goal is to remove the urine odor and neither will accomplish this, keep the latter for mixing drinks and the former for salads.

What you should use is an odor neutralizer specially made for removing, not covering up, urine odors. Manufactured under several brand names, they're available at most pet stores. The one I use is called Nature's Miracle.

FIDO REFUSES TO "GO" OUTDOORS

Occasionally, a dog will absolutely refuse to void outdoors. This may be a result of several factors. Fido may be so confused that he simply does not know where to put it anymore. He waits until no one is around, then relieves himself on the floor. The same problem may occur if Fido is too well paper-trained and refuses to go anywhere except on his pad or paper. Regardless of the reason, this can be very frustrating if you're Fido's owner and you've walked him outside for hours with no success.

There are many approaches that you can try in order to rectify the situation, but none of them will work with every dog. If Fido has been paper-trained, you can always try to bring the pad or paper outside, although often he'll just play with it or watch as the wind blows it down the block. Another approach is to take some of Fido's mess outside, place it where you want him to eliminate, then walk him in the same area. Hopefully, he'll recognize the familiar odor and respond accordingly. If he doesn't you'll have a lot of explaining to do to the neighbors who see you go through this little ritual!

If Fido's refusal to void gets really out of hand, you may want to consult with your vet regarding the use of infant glycerol suppositories.

The voiding problems outlined above are often the result of the confusion arising from utilizing paper-training as an intermediate step. That's why I recommend going directly to housebreaking if at all possible.

PAPER-TRAINING

Earlier in this chapter I discussed scenarios that called for the utilization of paper-training. Once you've decided that paper-training is the best approach in your situation, you should begin immediately.

Take great care to ensure that Fido learns quickly where he is permitted to go in the house. Many of the principles of the housebreaking process hold true for paper-training. The regulation of his system is a key factor. It will tip you off as to when Fido will have to eliminate. At that time he should be placed in his elimination area with his pad or paper. As in housebreaking, the proper cleaning of accidents is essential, and the proper diet and amount of water must be given.

To successfully paper-train Fido, a four-by-four-foot confinement area should be chosen, totally covered with pads or paper, and gated off. If you're using unprinted newspaper, use a thickness of approximately one quarter inch. Just as with housebreaking, most people prefer to use a linoleum- or tile-covered area such as the kitchen for easy cleanup. Whenever Fido may have to go, or whenever he is unsupervised, he should be placed in this area.

After a few days, a pattern should develop. It should become obvious that Fido is sleeping in one end of the area and voiding in the other. Once this pattern is established, you may gradually (every few days) begin to remove the pads or paper from the section Fido is sleeping in. Once this is successfully accomplished, increase the size of the confinement area every few days. The goal is to eventually give Fido the run of the house, with him returning to his pad or paper area whenever nature calls.

EASING FIDO'S TRANSITION
TO THE GREAT OUTDOORS

You may have chosen paper-training as a necessary intermediate step to housebreaking due to your own personal situation. Perhaps you have to work and just can't get home to supervise Fido during the day. Or perhaps your vet has told you to keep Fido indoors until he's completed his series of vaccinations. If your ultimate goal is to have Fido housebroken (relieving himself outdoors), there is something you can do to ease his transition to the great outdoors.

If you place a little grass and/or soil on his pad or paper, he's less likely to refuse to void when you take him outside.

THE ULTIMATE FORM OF PAPER-TRAINING—
THE LITTER BOX

If you live in an apartment or house without a yard, or work extremely long hours, and particularly if your four-footed best friend is one of the smaller breeds, litter-box training may be for you.

As an alternative to having Fido relieve himself on pads or papers on the floor in some area of your home, Fido can be taught to go in an uncovered litter box. Unlike cats, dogs do not require litter in the box. Instead, line the box with either unprinted newspaper or absorbent pads. These can be easily removed as they become soiled, and the litter box can be washed out on a regular basis.

Follow the same steps as outlined in the section on paper-training. Once Fido has established one end of his pad or paper area as his sleeping section and the other end as his potty, replace the pad or paper in his elimination area with the litter box. To encourage him to use the litter box, dab a little of his mess on the lining of the box. Place Fido in the litter box when you anticipate he needs to relieve himself. He should get the hang of it in no time.

ALL POTTY PROBLEMS
ARE NOT THE SAME

Potty problems take a variety of directions. Some of our four-footed best friends use the pads and paper or the outdoors most of the time, having only occasional accidents on the floor. Others are in the on-again, off-again category; it's fifty-fifty with them. Then there are the extremely sensitive hounds whose toilet habits can be disrupted by any emotional upheaval or major change within the family, such as divorce or a new baby. And then there are those dogs who just haven't a clue. These dogs simply prefer your most expensive Oriental rug or, heaven forbid, your pillow. I know how it is. You have my sympathy.

I'm lucky. Tige's a pro. He lets me know when nature calls by standing at the back door. He also has the patience (and the physical ability) to hold himself when his Pop is running a little late getting back home from work. Your four-footed best friend can be like that, too. Any dog can learn the finer points of potty etiquette.

BELIEVE IT OR NOT, FLUFFY IS
NOT TRYING TO BE SPITEFUL

Flabbergasted by Fluffy's behavior when she makes a deposit somewhere other than where she's supposed to? The main thing you need to remember is that 99.999 times out of 100, dogs are not spiteful. They really don't stay up at night thinking of ways to get even with you. They don't lounge around the house while you're out, contemplating the next way to aggravate you. In virtually every case there is a reason, or more likely a combination of reasons, for such a response. Potty problems are no exception.

THE HANSEL AND GRETEL SYNDROME

If you're wondering why Fluffy's little indiscretions occur on your pillow, perhaps when someone in the family is out of town, think about what I have termed the Hansel and Gretel syndrome. Dogs, like certain other animals, use their excrement as a means of sending out a message. First, the scent lets other dogs know they're coming close to Fluffy's turf. Second, the scent helps dogs find their way, just like the breadcrumbs Hansel and Gretel dropped on their journey through the forest. So when someone's out of the house and Fluffy's missing that family member, she may leave little accidents around as a means of helping her loved one find the way back home, particularly on things that strongly carry the person's scent. That's why pillows, comforters, and unwashed clothing are often prime targets. From your point of view it may look like intentional spite, because it seems to happen only when you're gone. But if you look at it from Fluffy's perspective, it takes on a whole new meaning.

SPECIAL TRICKS TO PREVENT POTTY PROBLEMS

Prevention is better than correction—at least, that's my philosophy about behavior. I'd much rather help a pet circumvent a problem than be corrective, authoritative, punitive, or dominant. I'm happier developing special little tricks that will ease Fluffy out of her bad behavior without her even realizing it.

In the following sections I describe the most common potty problems owners encounter plus tips on how to address them. If you're four-footed best friend is having potty problems, one or more of the following scenarios will sound familiar to you.

FLUFFY'S FAVORITE SPOTS—
IN YOUR HOME!

Has Fluffy decided that certain areas of your house are her preferred elimination spots? Most dogs will pick out one to three different areas where they prefer to soil. In the most severe cases, there may be a half-dozen hot spots. If you've had Fluffy checked by the vet and he or she has ruled out any physical problems, tried correcting her by confining her with her mess (see page 105), and used the proper cleaning agent and odor neutralizer, you should take this next step.

To repeat a point that I made earlier, dogs are clean animals. Remember how, in my section on paper-training, I described a pattern that develops—the puppy will use one end of his confinement area for sleeping and eating, and the other for elimination. In general, dogs won't eliminate in areas where they eat, play, or sleep. So let's use this knowledge to prevent Fluffy from soiling in the house (or in off-limits areas, if Fluffy is paper-trained). To accomplish this, begin by feeding Fluffy in the areas where she has been soiling.

Divide Fluffy's normal food portions between her regular dish and several paper plates. You should have one paper plate for each area being soiled. For example, if Fluffy's favorite areas for elimination are on your bed, on top of the dirty-laundry pile, and on your favorite Oriental rug, you should divide the meal into four parts. The regular feeding bowl should be left in its normal location and should contain one quarter of her meal. The remaining food should be divided into three parts. One plate should be placed on your bed (yes, on your bed!), another on the laundry pile, and the other on your Oriental rug. If you think it sounds disgusting to have these food dishes on places like your bed, I guarantee it's better than the alternative! Don't pick up the paper plates when Fluffy finishes the food, but leave them there as reminders. Of course, you'll remove the plate on your bed at bedtime, but be sure to put it back in the morning. Continue this process for a few weeks.

Once Fluffy has demonstrated she has broken her old habit, remove a plate for a day and then put it back in place. Wait a few days. Repeat that process a few times. When two or three weeks go by with no accidents, completely remove one of the plates. Wait a week. If there are still no lapses of bad behavior, remove the second plate. Wait a week. If everything's okay, remove the third, and so forth. Should Fluffy suffer a regression and again soil in those hot spots, it simply means you moved too quickly. Backtrack and start over, remaining at each step for a longer period of time. You have nothing to lose by moving ahead too slowly and everything to lose by moving too quickly.

If you're having a particularly tough time, you might try placing some of Fluffy's favorite toys, in addition to her food, in the areas where she is soiling. As a general rule, our four-footed friends don't like to eliminate in areas where they eat or play.

CHANGING FLUFFY FROM AN OUTDOOR DOG TO AN INDOOR DOG

How do you limit the confusion of an outdoor dog who must now learn to live and eliminate indoors? For instance, you've adopted a dog from the local humane society and discover that she hasn't a clue when it comes to using paper or pads or a litter box. Odds are she is accustomed to eliminating outdoors—usually on dirt or grass. To teach her to eliminate in a designated area of your home, place some dirt and grass plus some of her mess on the paper or pads or in the litter box. The grass, dirt, and mess remind and encourage her where to go when nature calls. She'll get the hang of it in no time. And when she does, be sure to give her lots of praise. Make her feel as if she's hit the lottery!

SENIOR FLUFFY HAS LAPSES

When an older dog forgets herself, there are probably more than a few senior-citizen-type problems creating the lapse in behavior. Golden-year canines are special, and I have a separate little spot in my heart just for them. They've given us the best years of their lives, and the least we can do is give them extra care when they need it most. For this reason I've devoted an entire section to senior citizen dogs (see page 260). Please refer to it for the old-timers' elimination needs as well as for advice on how to make their remaining time with us happy and healthy.

PRAISING FLUFFY

Praise, praise, praise Fluffy for every positive step she takes. The instant she's done what she's supposed to do where she's supposed to do it, go overboard with praise. Tell her she's wonderful, how pleased you are, and how she's the best thing that ever walked on four legs. Hug her. Pet her. Love her. Carry on like an idiot for a couple of minutes. With all this positive attention flying in her direction, Fluffy's bound to pick up on what you're asking. No quick pats on the head accompanied by blasé praise. If the only time Fluffy gets special attention is when you correct her, she'll continue doing whatever it takes to get that attention—even if it's negative attention. So accentuate the positive.

IF YOU MUST CORRECT FLUFFY . . .

As I said before, I'm not a fan of using corrections to change behavior. If you must correct Fluffy by confining her with her mess, leave her for twenty minutes only, coming back at two ten-minute intervals to say "no." Say "no" and only "no." Don't recite a whole speech about how upset you are and how she should wait until Daddy gets home. Too much attention to the problem is just as bad as not enough. At the end of the twenty minutes, stop. Forget about it, and don't hold any grudges.

By making Fluffy stay with her mess, you're telling her: "I don't care where you go in the house. If you make a mistake, you're just going to stay with it." It's like sending a kid to his room for twenty minutes to think about something wrong he said or did. With Fluffy, the only difference is that you're putting the accident with her to help remind her what she should be thinking about.

And please, don't rub her nose in it. That's humiliating. Don't bring her over to the spot and yell at her. All you're doing is telling her it's bad to go there in that particular spot. The next day she'll move a little to the left and go there, then move a little to the right and go there.

SOME WORDS FOR
MORAL SUPPORT

Generally speaking, the longer any habit has been in existence, the more time is needed to correct it. It really has little to do with the age of the dog or any other factor except for the length of time the problem has been a habit. The more ingrained the behavior, the longer it usually takes to reverse the procedure.

Whatever you do, don't become frustrated if Fluffy suffers one or more relapses. This is normal for the learning process. Just because everything is going along famously and you've patted yourself on the back for a job well done and then suffered a setback, don't give up! It is perfectly okay. Regressions should be expected. We often fail in our first, second, or third attempts to modify our behavior. However, in each case we come away having learned something that adds greatly to the possibility of success the next time around. The same principle applies to our four-footed best friends when they're learning something new or kicking an old bad habit.

LESSON NUMBER TWO: TEACHING FIDO TO WALK ON A LEASH

FIDO'S INTRODUCTION TO A LEASH AND COLLAR

Puppies do not always appreciate the introduction of a leash and collar into their lives. Their reactions may range from obstinacy to fearful submission. As with all training, you must carefully consider puppy Fido's attention span. It's important not to force him into an unpleasant experience, as his introduction to a leash and collar is very frequently the first taste of training. If puppy Fido is slow to respond, your harsh or hurried reaction may ruin forever Fido's enthusiasm for training.

WHY FIDO SHOULD BE TRAINED TO WALK ON A LEASH

I know some of you reading this are saying to yourselves, "What does he think we are? Morons? Of course Fido should learn to

walk on a leash." But, yes, folks, there are some people out there—often first-time dog owners—who assume that their dog does not have to learn how to walk on a leash because either Fido is an "indoor dog," one of the tiny breeds who has been paper- or litter-box trained and will live his entire life in a high-rise apartment, or Fido is an "outdoor dog" and will live his entire life on a multiacre property in the boondocks.

First, there's the obvious reason for teaching Fido to walk on a leash: Leashes give owners a secure means of control when dogs need to be moved from one environment to another. Even if Fido is strictly an indoor dog, you'll have to take him to the vet. This also goes for Fido if he lives out in a rural area with lots of land to roam on. Unless he's properly adjusted to a dog carrier (which is not always the case with the general dog population), it means dragging out the carrier and then playing hide-and-seek with Fido. The frightened hound will probably take one look at the carrier, realize what is about to take place, and hide under the nearest piece of furniture. Once you've dragged him out from under it (hopefully without getting nipped in the process), then comes the dreaded moment when Fido gets stuffed in the box. Mind you, I'm not advocating stuffing Fido into the carrier, but that's what generally happens with anxious dogs and their owners. By this point, Fido has spread each of his four amazingly steel-like legs in four totally different directions, making his approach into the carrier sort of like fitting fifteen college students into one telephone booth.

Okay! So you've finally got him securely in the carrier. You're both panting and sweating, and your hearts are racing. You know this can't be the right thing to do—it's upset both of you so. One of several possible scenarios unfolds next. Fido is either howling and whining or he's scrunched up in the corner, hugging the back of the carrier so tightly he might as well be wallpapered to the container. Of course, both scenarios are accompanied by shaking and other nervous reactions—tail between the legs, heavy panting, and in some cases, spontaneous urination or bowel movements. Is this good? I think not. Score one point for teaching Fido to walk on a leash.

Another very important reason for teaching Fido to walk on a leash is avoiding plain old boredom. Dogs are too intelligent to be expected to live in the same home, surrounded by the same four walls, watching the same soap operas, day in and day out, 365 days a year, for the next ten to eighteen years of their lives. The same applies to dogs whose lives are spent on their owners' property. While their territory may seem a bit more interesting than an apartment, being on it day in and day out is still tantamount to a jail sentence of cruel and unusual punishment. Boredom is a key factor in the majority of the behavioral problems I encounter; it is healthier for Fido to experience the joys of the world. After all, he wants to go with you. He doesn't want to be alone all day, never visiting Grandma or seeing the cousins. Fido wants to know why he can't go on a Sunday drive with the rest of the family or on a quick trip to the hardware store. If Fido is trained to walk on a leash, he can experience the outside world with you, and his boredom can be greatly decreased.

Fear of escape has a lot to do with preventing us from taking Fido on special outings. A leash gives us the control. Remember, no matter how well trained your dog is, he should never be off his leash in a strange environment.

Finally, you never know when the need to have Fido stay with someone else will arise. Perhaps an out-of-town trip will leave you with no option but to have Fido stay with someone else. What if you have to spend a prolonged period of time in the hospital, or, heaven forbid, you are no longer able to care for Fido? His chances of being adopted are far greater if he has been trained to walk on a leash. So do yourself and your four-footed best friend a favor: Train him to walk on a leash.

STEP-BY-STEP INSTRUCTIONS FOR STEPPING OUT WITH FIDO

STEP ONE: PURCHASING THE RIGHT OUTFIT

SELECTING THE RIGHT COLLAR

For puppies, I recommend using a lightweight buckle-type collar made of nylon. Most pet shops carry a line of inexpensive puppy collars well suited for this purpose, enabling you to replace the collar frequently as your puppy grows larger. Great care should be taken to ensure a properly fitted collar. It should be tight enough to prevent it from slipping over the puppy's head but loose enough to slip two fingers underneath it.

When Fido is full grown, I recommend using a rolled leather collar. The collar's rolled design will prevent it from making the hair on Fido's neck become matted.

A WORD ABOUT TRAINING COLLARS

Because you're starting puppy Fido's training at a very early age, a training collar, often referred to as a choke collar by people who are not knowledgeable in its proper use, is totally unnecessary.

The only time you might consider utilizing a training collar is if Fido is fully grown and has never had any basic training. Remember, as far as I'm concerned, the old adage is wrong— You *can* teach an old dog new tricks!

The training collar, as its name implies, is used for corrections during Fido's obedience training. It is not a substitute for Fido's regular rolled leather collar that he wears when he's not in a training session. When attached to the leash, the training collar enables you to quickly jerk the leash to the side then release it quickly. The noise of the chain of the training collar alerts the dog that he has erred and that he should keep his attention on the handler. *Never* leave this collar on when the dog is unsupervised. It is easy for him to catch one end and hang himself.

If you do opt to use a training collar, its proper length is determined by measuring around the dog's neck and adding two inches. The collar should be placed on the dog so that when jerked it releases immediately. The easiest way to avoid error is to place the collar to form the letter "P." With the dog in front of you, place the collar over his head. By doing it this way you will always be correct.

Finally, never ever use a prong collar or electric shock collar. As far as I'm concerned, people who use such devices should try wearing them themselves!

SELECTING THE RIGHT LEASH

When training Fido, I recommend using a six-foot training leash. At this length, Fido can enjoy some freedom while you still maintain control. The best materials for a training leash are leather, nylon, or cotton web. While all of these are lightweight, I personally prefer the cotton web, because it's less slippery and easier to grasp. In my opinion, chain leads are unsuitable for training.

The strength of puppy Fido's leash is not nearly as important as it is if Fido is a powerful sixty-pound dog. However, puppy Fido's leash still shouldn't be flimsy. Be a good consumer and check the construction, particularly around the handle and clip areas. Is it stitched well? Are these areas reinforced with extra stitching or with grommets? Check for loose strings. Often the lesser-quality items are not finished well (telltale thread ends are the biggest tip-off). Don't be afraid to pull, pick, or use your fingernails to check a product. I'm not suggesting you ruin the shopkeeper's merchandise, but if you notice within a few seconds of your product-testing that the leash shows some wear and tear, I guarantee that Fido, whether he's a puppy or full grown, will have it looking like a disaster in no time. Worse, it may not be safe, and may break apart when you least expect it.

Next, take a good hard look at the clip—that's the area attaching the leash to the collar. Leash fasteners should be sturdy, not flimsy like a cheap key ring. Be sure the weight of the clip is not too heavy around your puppy's neck, yet is adequate enough to provide the necessary safety.

Play around with the clip's snap mechanism. It should open and close properly, not too easily but not with too much difficulty. And it should close tightly. After you test a few different clips on several varieties of leashes, you'll see what I mean about the difference. It's obvious once you know what you're looking for.

STEP TWO: FIDO'S INTRODUCTION TO A COLLAR

At first only the lightweight collar should be placed on puppy Fido's neck. This should be done for only a few minutes at a time. Each time the collar is on Fido, be sure you do something special, such as bringing out his favorite toy or feeding him his favorite treat (but in moderation—I'd much rather you give him hugging and loving than food rewards). And don't forget lots of praise, too. Let Fido think that every time he wears the collar something wonderful is going to happen. We all learn through association—and dogs are no different. Have Fido wear the collar for short intervals, gradually increasing the time periods as he appears more comfortable. Within a matter of days, Fido will be trotting around the house paying no real attention to the collar.

The same procedure applies when introducing full-grown Fido to a collar. The only difference is that you will be using either the rolled leather or training collar.

STEP THREE: FIDO'S INTRODUCTION TO A LEASH

Once Fido—whether he's a puppy or full grown—reaches the point where he's comfortable with the collar, it's time to introduce the leash itself. Use the same type of positive reinforcement you used when acclimating him to the collar. Be sure to watch his reaction. If he is fearful, take the leash off and then praise him. Repeat the procedure several times, for short intervals, always in conjunction with some pleasurable activity. Allow him to walk where he pleases, dragging the leash behind him. Of course, be sure to supervise him in case his leash gets caught on anything. Continue these short intervals for several days if necessary, gradually increasing the time he's on the leash, until Fido shows no visible negative response to the leash.

A REMINDER—PATIENCE IS A VIRTUE

Some dogs, puppies in particular, will appear totally unreceptive to the leash—actually yelping and screaming at it. In this case, patience is key to Fido's adjustment. How would you feel if all of a sudden someone placed something around your neck, then added a six-foot-long "snake" that followed you wherever you went? Not only does this snake follow you around, it (and its clip) also adds weight you're not accustomed to dragging around. I wouldn't be too thrilled myself!

That's why it's so important to watch Fido's reaction to the leash and to praise him even while removing it. If Fido's reaction is a negative one, check to see that his collar is not too tight by slipping two fingers under it. Once you're sure his collar is comfortable, try removing the clip from the leash and attaching only the clip to his collar. By attaching only the clip, you will let him have the feeling of weight without his having to contend with the clumsiness of the leash. After a day or so, Fido should be trotting around without a problem.

Once Fido appears to be comfortable with the collar and clip, it's time to reintroduce the leash. Do it in conjunction with his favorite activity, favorite treat, and lots of hugs and praise. Let him associate the leash with fun and good things. Getting down on the floor to his eye level will add to his sense of security. Again, be sure to watch Fido's reaction. If he's fearful, take the leash off and praise him. Repeat this procedure several times, always for short periods of time, and always praising him—no matter what his response is. It's at times like these that patience is definitely a virtue! But I promise you, by being patient, kind, and taking it a little at a time, you will soon have Fido trotting around on the leash—not giving it a second thought.

WHAT IF PUPPY FIDO USES HIS LEASH AS A TEETHING RING?

It's not uncommon for puppy Fido to try to chew on his leash. After all, he may be at that uncomfortable teething stage. If you catch your four-footed best friend chewing on his leash, give him other options. I recommend using frozen rawhide bones (see page 171). When Fido starts to chew on his leash, offer him the bones instead. He'll enjoy their taste better than the leash, and their cool temperature will be much more soothing to his painful gums.

If you try this technique and Fido still insists on chewing on his leash, you can spray the leash with Bitter Apple or Bitter Lime. Widely available at pet stores, these nontoxic products leave an unpleasant taste where applied. Spray the leash, and Fido will get the idea in no time. Because these products evaporate rapidly, it may be necessary to reapply them often. Of course, be sure to read and follow the manufacturers' directions.

STEP FOUR: LET FIDO DECIDE WHERE YOU'RE GOING

Once Fido's comfortable with the leash and collar, it's time to start walking together. Or, should I say, start walking where he wants to. Pick up the end of the leash and actually follow him around. Don't try to get him to walk in the direction you want. Just follow. Practice this for a few days. When he looks comfortable, you're ready to teach the little student to walk with you.

STEP FIVE: GOING WHERE YOU WANT TO GO

Once Fido gets the idea of walking around with you sheepishly following behind, it's time to teach him to go where you want to go. While giving Fido so much verbal encouragement that the neighbors think it's time to commit you to the local asylum, begin walking in the direction of your choice. Your voice should be sweet, high-pitched (men will need to practice this), and exciting. Fido will probably take a few steps in your direction then put on the brakes. Firmly placing all four paws on the ground, he'll give you a look that translates as "Go ahead, just try to move me." Then he'll dig in for the battle of the wills. Don't think that because he's stopped dead in his tracks you need to drag and pull him. If you do, you'll quickly learn a basic law of doggy physics: The more an owner pulls in one direction, the more the dog resists and pulls in the other.

MY SECRET WEAPON FOR DOGS WHO
WON'T BUDGE AN INCH

When Fido's glued to the floor and refuses to move, a special technique needs to be employed, called the little tug and release. With the least amount of effort, give the leash the lightest possible tug and then quickly release the tug so that the leash hangs loosely. If Fido doesn't move, repeat this procedure several times in a row, taking a four- or five-second pause between each tug. While you're doing this, continue with excited high-pitched verbal encouragement.

Don't be afraid to get down on your hands and knees to encourage Fido from his eye level. Don't be disillusioned if your stubborn four-footed best friend only moves six inches or so on the first dozen attempts. Keep at it, as any good teacher would, and you'll start to notice little breakthroughs. One day he'll just get up and walk around with you. You'll celebrate, pat yourself on the back, and call the relatives at work and let them know what a genius dog you have. Then, of course, the next day Fido will look at you with that old give-me-a-break, I-know-you-can't-be-serious-look. When this happens—and it's bound to happen—don't despair. It's 100 percent normal for intelligent animals; they'll test the limits to see what they can get away with. Just keep plugging away with the little-tug-and-release technique.

DON'T MISUSE THIS TECHNIQUE

Let's review the important points of the little-tug-and-release method again, because applying this technique incorrectly may actually discourage Fido from walking. The tug should be ever so gentle, not a pull and not a drag but the slightest little tug, and must be followed by an immediate release. There should be no tension on the collar. Wait several seconds between each tug and release. As you work on this procedure, it helps to actually say to yourself "tug-release, tug-release, tug-release." For whatever reason, probably dating back to the old drag-the-dog-if-he-doesn't-want-to-walk approach that so many early training books advocated, owners forget to release after the tug. That's exactly what we don't want. We're not looking to place constant pressure on Fido, but just to give the gentlest little nudge in the right direction. Practice every day for a few minutes. It's not necessary, and it's not even a good idea, to have a lengthy once-a-day training session when Fido is learning to walk on a leash. It's much better for him, and more likely to fit into your busy schedule, for you to practice a few minutes here and there. Keep up the praise; it's easy to forget, particularly if Fido is a little slow to learn. The more frustrated you become, the less praise you'll probably use—the direct opposite of what should be done. Reluctant dogs need all the praise and confidence-building they can get.

If frustration does strike, don't take it out on Fido. Go beat up your pillow, then make yourself a cup of tea, or maybe even pour yourself a glass of wine. Then take a much-needed break and try again.

STEP SIX: STEPPING OUT WITH FIDO

You and Fido probably went through the five preceding steps either in the secure and familiar surroundings of your home or your own backyard. Now it's time to tackle the great outdoors (provided that if Fido is a puppy, he's completed his necessary vaccinations and received your vet's okay to venture off your property). If Fido's never been outside, you'll have to take it a bit slow. There's a big, frightening world out there, full of all sorts of strange sights, smells, and noises. So before expecting him to go for a long walk around the neighborhood, be sure he feels comfortable outside. Sometimes the best plan of action is to do nothing, meaning you simply go outside with Fido on a leash and sit on the stoop. Just let Fido see and hear the world go by. This is particularly important for city dogs and dogs who live in high-traffic areas. You'll know when Fido has adapted to his new environment. He'll develop a relaxed look and become curious about the new sights, possibly even wandering off a little to explore. When this occurs—and with some dogs this happens immediately, while with others it takes some time—it's time to take him for the smallest of walks. Just as you did during Fido's first introduction to wearing a leash, let Fido take you where he wants to go (provided it's not into traffic!). Follow him until he gets the idea of walking outdoors on a leash. Once he does, encourage him to walk where you want to go. Lots of encouragement and praise are needed here—so don't be surprised when passersby throw you some pretty strange glances! Ignore them, keep up the praise, and soon you and Fido will be going for long walks together.

HELPFUL HINTS IF FIDO'S THE NERVOUS TYPE

If your four-footed best friend is a little skittish and the big, frightening world out there seems a bit overwhelming to him, there are a couple of things you can do to make his transition to the great outdoors easier.

The first (and this applies even if Fido is not the nervous type) is to use good old-fashioned common sense when it comes to where and when you introduce Fido to the outside world. If your street is a busy, heavily traveled one, you may want to choose a time of day when it's quieter. Very early in the morning or later in the evening may be good times. Perhaps weekends, particularly Sundays, are quieter. If you live near a school, you may want to avoid introducing Fido to the great outdoors at dismissal time, when there's the distraction of kids heading home from school. You know your neighborhood best, so plan ahead before Fido's first adventure into the big world outside your door.

The second is to desensitize him to outside noise before he actually ventures out of your home. Softly play a tape recording or sound-effects record of trucks, sirens, traffic, etc. Gradually increase the volume over a period of days and weeks as Fido seems relaxed with the current level of sound. This technique is particularly valuable for fully grown dogs who are having a hard time making the transition from a quiet, suburban environment to the big city.

A FEW FINAL WORDS OF ADVICE

Don't be frustrated if you or your canine student hits a snag during the learning process. If you find that you're having trouble with any of the previous steps, it simply means you've advanced a little too quickly. Go back to the steps preceding the problem and spend a little more time perfecting the weak areas. I promise you that with a little patience and a lot of encouragement, praise, and hugs, you and your four-footed best friend will graduate together!

CANINE KINDERGARTEN, PHASE TWO: THE DOGGY ALPHABET

Now that Fido and Fluffy have mastered their first lessons, it's time to go on to phase two of their educations. In other words, it's time for them to learn their ABCs.

THE DOGGY ALPHABET

In order to best communicate with Fido, there are some basic commands both you and he should know. Just as a child cannot learn to read without knowing his ABCs, Fido needs to learn his own version of the alphabet. Fido's ABCs consist of the basic obedience commands of "heel," "sit," "stay," "down," and "come." By mastering these basics through verbal commands and hand signals, both you and he will better be able to communicate and enjoy a happy, rewarding relationship.

WHY OBEDIENCE-TRAIN?

Obedience training consists of a series of exercises designed to make Fido and Fluffy better citizens and companions. You'll use each of the commands—heel, sit, stay, down, and come—in practical everyday situations. For instance, Fido will walk quietly by your side in a crowd, sit down automatically when you stop, and wait patiently when you leave him on a stay command. Fluffy will come instantly the first time that you call her, and will lie down when asked to do so.

You say that this doesn't sound like something your four-footed best friend can do? C'mon, give him more credit than that! If he's a puppy, follow the steps described in the following sections and he'll surprise you. If he's full grown and hasn't mastered his ABCs, it's only because he has not been properly trained. Remember my motto: You *can* teach an old(er) dog new tricks!

FIDO WENT TO OBEDIENCE CLASS
AND HE STILL WON'T LISTEN

In many ways our four-footed best friends are just like our children. Some are lazy, some excitable, some anxious to please, while others exhibit independent determination. Others are timid or reserved, while still others are gregarious extroverts. And all of them learn at different rates. Our school systems generally take these factors into consideration by offering different levels of study, including remedial classes and special study groups. Unfortunately, most canine obedience classes don't. Instead they lump together ten to twenty dogs, often of varying ages and abilities, into one class and apply the same training techniques to all of them. As a result of this, some canine pupils will do well while others will fail miserably. Just the fact that there are other dogs and people in the class can be too much of a distraction for a dog that hasn't been properly socialized.

As far as I'm concerned, any dog with normal intelligence and caring owners can be taught basic obedience. The methods vary slightly with each individual dog. The major difference is the addition of even more praise and encouragement for a less secure dog. Remember, you know your dog's personality best.

THE KEYS TO SUCCESSFUL OBEDIENCE TRAINING

PRAISE

Praise is the incentive for Fido. He should receive it each and every time that he behaves properly. Even more important, he should be praised and reassured after each and every correction. Note that I use the term "correction" as opposed to "punishment." Correction must always be administered constructively and consistently. More on obedience correction appears on page 134.

CONSISTENCY

Consistency is paramount. Be sure to use the same word to mean the same thing each and every time that the word is used. For instance, the word "down" means to lie down and should not also be used to mean no jumping on people or furniture. Using the same word in two different contexts can be very confusing to Fido. Consistency is not just limited to the words you use. You must be consistent in your corrections. By allowing Fido to not obey a command one time and chastising him for the same action the next time, you're sending mixed signals to him and undermining your control.

KEEP IT SIMPLE

One-word or simple commands are best. Most dogs cannot understand statements such as "Please, Fido, get off the couch, because you know Daddy doesn't like that." Try to choose words that do not sound like other commands. "Go" and "no" can be confusing.

WHAT ABOUT HAND SIGNALS?

We'll be using verbal commands as the basis for teaching Fido his ABCs. The use of hand signals is therefore optional. If you do opt to use them, realize that your dog will be seeing your hand from a much lower vantage point (unless he's a Great Dane!). You may find it helpful to practice the hand signals in front of a mirror prior to executing them with your four-footed best friend.

If you do use hand signals, they must be used *simultaneously* with the verbal command during Fido's lessons. I can't emphasize strongly enough the importance of doing both in unison during Fido's training. Here, again, it'll pay off to practice beforehand. Ultimately, after Fido has mastered his ABCs, you'll be able to eliminate one or the other (the verbal command or hand signal) and rely strictly on the remaining one as a means of communicating with him.

THE THREE BIGGEST TRAINING MISTAKES TO AVOID

1. *Never Hit Your Dog.* My approach of hugs, kisses, and praise will accomplish a lot more and is certainly more humane. Hitting a dog can make him fearful of your hand, a problem that is better known as hand shyness. Hand shyness

creates many difficulties—the least of which can occur during obedience training if the dog is expected to respond to hand signals. A much more serious result of hand shyness is possible aggression by the dog toward people—especially toward children. I can't tell you how many children have been bitten as a result of putting their hands in the face of a dog fearful of being hit.

2. *Never Use "No" with Your Dog's Name.* In other words, don't say "No, Fido" when correcting him. Fido's name should always be used for positives. Your four-footed best friend's spoken name should always elicit a positive response from him and will often be used preceding a command for some action or motion on his part (i.e., "Fido, come"). The idea is to have him obey happily and without reservation. Remember, to successfully accomplish this, a positive attitude and an excited but sweet voice tone on your part are mandatory.

3. *Never Reprimand Your Dog for Not Coming When He Is Called, and Never Call Your Dog to You to Correct Him.* After all, if someone called you and upon arriving you were hit or scolded, you wouldn't be too eager to respond the next time. If you must correct Fido, go to him to do so.

THE TRAINING SESSIONS— WHEN AND HOW LONG?

Remember that overtraining a dog is as harmful as undertraining him. Avoid the hottest time of the day and and before and after meals. Short, happy training sessions followed by play periods will create a happy worker. Keep the work fast-paced and demanding for the period of Fido's greatest attention span. This will keep him from becoming bored or sloppy and will not allow him time to become distracted. Of course, use common sense. A puppy's attention span will more than likely be shorter than that of an older dog. Finally, take your own attention span and attitude into consideration. Be sure that you have the time, patience, and concentration needed to make it a positive session.

NOW IT'S TIME FOR YOU TO LEARN: THE OBEDIENCE CORRECTION

Before you embark on your first obedience session with Fido, there's something you must learn and practice—the obedience correction. This jerk of the leash is used to indicate to Fido that he has made a mistake. The development of a correct jerk coupled with an effective "no!" is the most important concept in obedience training. Without it, basic obedience—Fido's mastery of the doggy alphabet—will never be firmly established. Therefore, it'll pay to spend some extra time on the development of the "jerk and no."

PERFECTING THE OBEDIENCE CORRECTION

With only a few exceptions, the leash is never to be jerked without an accompanying verbal "no!" You don't want to become overly dependent on the leash as the correction. It's much better to begin even the earliest stages of training with an emphasis on voice-controlled responses instead. So remember, every jerk must be accompanied by an authoritative "no!"

The timing of the jerk and no is crucial. Ideally, the jerk and no should be used just *before* Fido has committed himself to a particular action. For instance, if Fido has the tendency to jump on people as they enter your home, anticipate this and use the jerk and no just as soon as Fido shows the first signs of jumping. Ideally the jerk and no would be best timed just as Fido's legs are first lifted off the floor, not after he is in full flight, pouncing on the person.

After a jerk-and-no correction has been given, the tension on the leash should be released *immediately*. Never pull, yank, or tug Fido. Steady pressure on his collar is not the correct approach; a quick jerk and an immediate release is.

IMPLEMENTING THE OBEDIENCE CORRECTION— WHEN FIDO WON'T RESPOND

I'm sure at one time or another we've all witnessed an owner attempting to train a dog who just doesn't seem to respond. Over and over the owner will command his pupil to "Sit! Sit! Sit!" without the desired response.

When practicing a previously learned command with an unresponsive pupil, I find that to continue repeating the command is counterproductive. In fact, this type of repetition often results in a dog that does not find it necessary to respond to the command the first time around. If you're absolutely positive that Fido understands the command, give the command once. If there is no response within a few seconds, correct him with a jerk and no. If there is still no response within a few seconds, repeat the jerk and no. This should be repeated a third time if necessary. Then, and only then, should the command be given again if Fido has not responded, taking into consideration that he may now have forgotten the original command.

HEEL

A dog walking properly at your side can be one of life's little pleasures. Flying down the street behind Fido or crawling along at a snail's pace can be both embarrassing and dangerous. Teaching him to walk correctly at your side, to heel as it is commonly called, will greatly enhance your relationship with your four-footed best friend. By following the step-by-step instructions given here, the learning process will be enjoyed by both you and your dog.

LABRADORS AND LHASAS ON THE LEFT

No matter what the breed, heeling consists of Fido walking with his shoulder close to your left knee. Why the left side? There are several theories, but my personal favorite is that most people being right-handed carry packages, newspapers, and the like on their right side. It becomes a matter of common sense to keep Fido on the left.

HEEL—A COMMAND, NOT A CONSTANT RESPONSE

There is no need to make Fido heel constantly. After all, if I'm walking my dog to let him do his thing, I don't want him peeing on my foot! However, at times it will be necessary for him to walk in the heel position. When out for a leisurely stroll, Fido should be able to walk in front of you, behind you, or to the side of you, provided he's not pulling. But when given the command to heel, Fido should immediately go into that position. "Heel" should be taught as a command, not as a constant response. Put yourself in Fido's position—never to be able to walk at the pace you wish, or allowed to turn around to get a good sniff of that sexy French poodle with the fancy clip and the expensive perfume!

THE PROPER USE OF A LEASH

Since a six-foot training leash should be used throughout most of Fido's lessons in the doggy alphabet, its proper use is important. Many people will take a six-foot leash and wrap it around their hand until only about one foot is left for their dog. These people brag about how well their dog is walking, while poor Fido looks up with his eyes popping and his tongue hanging out, gasping for air. When the six-foot leash is used properly, it gives Fido the chance to make mistakes and receive the proper corrections. It's a lot more humane than a constant choking session!

WHERE

When teaching Fido to heel, it'll be beneficial to work in situations that you'll both have to face on a daily basis, such as children playing baseball or hockey in the street, bicycles streaking down the block, the neighbors' crooning poodles, or the ultimate distraction—a delivery boy with a bag full of Chinese food! At first, you may start Fido's lessons in a less distracting area, such as your yard. However, once Fido demonstrates that he has a basic understanding of what he is expected to do, he should be worked at schoolyards, shopping centers, and other high-traffic areas that present him with many distractions. Fido should be exposed to cars, motorcycles, and sirens. Remember—at first he will be more likely to be nervous, but gradual exposure will surely overcome this.

FANCY FOOTWORK

Believe it or not, *your* feet are key in the proper handling of your dog. After all, it's the footwork of his owner that cues Fido to the desired response. Since people walk at different paces, it's important for Fido to learn fast, slow, and normal paces. For instance, if you're making a left turn and Fido crosses in front of you, a collision is inevitable! So when practicing turns with your dog, remember to pivot on your right foot when making a left turn. Pivot on your left when making a right turn. You'll find that practicing in front of a mirror—no matter how silly you might feel doing so—will certainly be helpful.

Heel: The About-Turn Method

TEACHING FIDO TO HEEL— THE ABOUT-TURN METHOD

The method that I've found most successful for teaching the heel command is the about-turn method. The about turn enables you to keep Fido's attention while he's learning to heel. By following the steps described below, you and Fido will become pros at the heel command.

1. Once you're sure that Fido's collar is on properly, hold his leash with the loop over your right thumb. A portion of the leash drops into your right hand, with your thumb and index finger pressing on it. Practice releasing and tightening your fingers so that the leash easily slides or stops at will.

Your left hand shouldn't be on the leash. Your right hand should fall directly at your side.

2. Keeping your eyes straight ahead, step off on your left foot. Your left foot will serve as a guide and will cue Fido, who will be standing at your left side.

3. Using his name first, give the command to heel. "Fido, heel." Remember, heel is a motion command, and the use of Fido's name prior to the command will grab his attention. At this point, the tone of your voice is key. The heel command must be authoritative and encouraging at the same time.

4. It is more than likely that, once in motion, Fido will forge out in front of you. As soon as this occurs, give a short, quick corrective jerk and no, stamp your left foot lightly on the ground, make an about-face turn, and repeat, "Fido, heel."

The key here is to continue making about-face turns each and every time Fido forges out ahead of you. You must remain in constant motion—don't stop. If you do stop, Fido has won.

Now I know what you're thinking: "Hey, wait a minute. If I follow Warren's advice, my dog and I won't get very far!" Actually, you're right. It's possible that you and Fido won't travel more than a few steps on your first attempts. But take heart. As with anything else, practice makes perfect.

Remember that dogs have a limited attention span. So fifteen-minute practice sessions are ideal—with occasional longer lessons thrown in, perhaps twice weekly. And don't forget the praise and encouragement. I want to hear a lot of "That's a good boy, Fido. Come on, Fido!"

HOW THE ELEMENTS OF THE ABOUT-TURN METHOD WORK

The command "heel" tells Fido what he's supposed to do. The correction tells him that he has made a mistake. The stamping of your left foot gets Fido's attention where it is supposed to be, and the repetition of the command keeps the lesson in perspective. The leash is held in one hand only—your right hand. If two hands are used on the leash, the tendency to hold back your dog is greater, which doesn't give him the opportunity to make the error and learn from his mistake.

It's to your benefit to keep Fido's body language and personality in mind when working with him. For instance, if Fido tends to crowd or nudge up alongside of you, it's possible that he's looking for a little more praise and attention. Be sure to take the time to give Fido the positive attention he's seeking. Taking a break in the lesson for some love and affection will improve your dog's working routine.

PROBLEMS WITH THE HEEL COMMAND

CROWDING

If Fido continues to crowd despite the praise and attention, corrective measures may be necessary. Crowding may be caused by you making eye contact with Fido. Eye contact makes him look up at you, and this will in turn cause him to walk at an angle—hence, crowding. In some instances this can be rectified easily if you simply keep your eyes straight forward. In the most extreme circumstances, a correction may be necessary. About turns to the left may be very helpful for stopping this problem. Continual left turns are enough of a surprise to keep your dog in the proper heel position. In general, crowding is not that major of a problem and can be resolved without the correction.

LAGGING

Another problem inherent in heeling is lagging. In this case, Fido plays anchor when taken outside. In this situation, your enthusiasm can make all the difference in the world. Talk to your dog, slap your side, promise him anything. "Heel, heel, heel" can be very boring for both you and Fido, so the conversation must be mutually agreeable and stimulating. "Fido, *heel*. C'mon fella, that's a good boy."

However, if the enthusiastic approach doesn't seem to resolve the problem, corrections may be used. Never jerk your dog forward. This causes even more tension, thus creating a tug-of-war. The best way to correct a lagger is via the use of the stay command (see page 150). With Fido sitting at the heel position, give the stay and take two large steps forward. Start the heel from this position, which will entice the dog to run and catch up with you. After all, nobody likes to be left behind!

Another way to cure a lagging dog is to turn about to your left as previously described. This will prevent you from becoming entangled with Fido. Right turns with the lagger will only get you all wound up in his leash. In contrast, a left turn will bring Fido out to the correct side so that you may continue walking.

FORGING

Next there is the forging dog, which is the opposite of the lagger. If Fido pulls you down the block, wraps you around telephone poles, or makes you trip up and down curbs, then you need to concentrate more on the heel. Place emphasis on the about turn, making sure that you execute the corrective jerk properly.

A FINAL WORD OF ADVICE

Remember, when teaching the heel command, or any other command, don't expect your dog to respond immediately. Many people read books on dog training and expect perfection. Unless you can teach your dog to read these books, you must be patient and consistent! If any lesson becomes frustrating—and some will—stop, and begin again later. After all, any short temper on your part will jeopardize your dog's positive response.

SIT

Sit is the one command that most owners think they already have mastered. It's not unusual to hear an owner say "Sit, Sit, Sit!" and to see the owner's "magic wand" index finger pushing at the dog's rear end. Then there are the other owners, who, after offering the dog a piece of cheese or some other tasty tidbit, turn proudly and exclaim, "See, what did I tell you? He's a genius!" What are these owners going to do when they're outdoors and Fido's out of reach, or they simply don't have a piece of food handy, and the dog no longer feels the need to respond?

THE WRONG APPROACHES

The preceding scenarios illustrate two of the wrong ways to teach Fido the sit command. Another well-known but possibly damaging method of teaching sit is to force Fido by pushing down on his hindquarters. Sometimes this will cause him to turn angrily to see whose hand is where it doesn't belong. After all, what would your reaction be if someone pushed you on your rear end? This approach can cause negative feelings that carry over into the rest of Fido's basic training.

THE CORRECT APPROACH—THE TUCK METHOD

I recommend the tuck method of teaching the sit. By following the steps outlined below you'll have your four-footed best friend (whether a puppy or an adult) sitting like a pro.

1. Have Fido stand lengthwise in front of you (you are facing his side, with his head to your right). Depending on his size, it may be necessary for you to kneel.
2. Holding his leash in your right hand, place your left hand on his legs just below his rear end and just above his stifles (knee joint).
3. Use your left hand and arm to place slow but gradual pressure on Fido, while giving the sit command.
4. As Fido sits, praise him profusely.

The key here is to give the verbal sit command simultaneously with the tuck, so that Fido begins to associate the word with the action you desire him to perform.

Depending on the dog, this may have to be repeated ten times or one hundred times. Keep in mind that several short sessions of fifteen minutes each will be the most beneficial, since the attention span of many of our four-footed best friends is relatively short. Don't assume that longer lessons will expedite Fido's training. Chances are that you will accomplish just the opposite!

*Sit: The
Tuck Method*

IF FIDO'S HAVING A PROBLEM WITH THE SIT

If Fido appears to be reluctant to sit or seems uncomfortable in the sitting position, a quick visit to the vet might be in order. Sometimes it could be as simple as having his anal glands cleaned. If it is physiological, have the problem corrected and continue your training. If it is psychological, take the proverbial "two steps backward" to ensure that Fido knows what you are doing.

THE FINAL STEP—THE SIT WITHOUT THE TUCK

Once you are confident that Fido is starting to catch on to the idea, you should give the verbal command to sit without using your hand to tuck. If he does not respond, and you're sure that he knows what is expected of him, you may start using the obedience correction described on page 134.

Once you have accomplished the sit command with about an 80 percent response on Fido's part, you're ready to incorporate the sit with the heel command—the automatic sit.

THE AUTOMATIC SIT

To the average person, the automatic sit sounds very impressive. The automatic sit is simply what its name implies. When heeling, Fido will sit when he comes to a stop without being told to do so. There are many practical uses for the automatic sit. For instance, prior to crossing a busy intersection, it is important for both your and his safety that Fido sits. It'll also be more pleasant for you (and Fido) if he sits while you're chatting with your friend or waiting for the kids' school bus.

TEACHING THE AUTOMATIC SIT

Prior to teaching the automatic sit, you should review the section on the sit command. If you or your dog are not proficient with this command, your attempts at the automatic sit will be disastrous!

Assuming you and Fido have mastered the sit command, here are the steps for teaching the automatic sit.

1. Begin with Fido sitting while in the heel position.
2. Start walking and give the heel command.
3. After a few steps, come to a slow, gradual stop. Remember—dogs don't have disc brakes!
4. Upon stopping, command Fido to sit. Make sure the command is given authoritatively.
5. Once Fido sits, be sure to praise him.
6. Start walking, again giving the heel command.
7. Repeat steps 3, 4, 5, and 6 several times, sometimes saying sit and sometimes not. Use the verbal command on a variable basis so Fido gets the idea of what's expected.

MAKING THE SIT AUTOMATIC— ELIMINATING THE VERBAL COMMAND ENTIRELY

When you find that Fido is sitting each and every time you give the sit command, you should be able to eliminate the spoken "sit" after coming to a stop. If, upon stopping, Fido does not automatically sit, and you doubt he will, use the basic obedience correction (the jerk) without any verbal correction. If three corrections produce no improvement, you must assume that Fido has no idea what you are doing. Backtrack to the earlier steps for a few minutes, then try again. All of a sudden Fido will sit after two or three corrections, and in a few more minutes he will sit with no corrections at all. Voilà! The automatic sit.

STAY

The stay command is a very practical, essential part of Fluffy's mastery of the doggy alphabet. This important command simply means that Fluffy should remain in a stationary position when commanded to do so. Although it can be applied when Fluffy is in any number of positions, we'll start by teaching it to her in the sit position using the following steps.

1. Begin with Fluffy sitting at your left side in the heel position, while you hold her leash in your right hand.
2. If you're using hand signals, use your left hand to give the hand signal for the stay. Your fingers should be pointing toward the ground, with the palm of the hand toward Fluffy.
3. Give the verbal command "stay" (simultaneously with the hand signal if you're using it). Because Fluffy is expected to remain stationary for a period of time, the command should be verbalized in an elongated manner. If it aids your elongation, visualize the letters "S-T-A-Y" in your mind as you're saying it. Do not use Fluffy's name with the stay command, because this is a stationary command—you're not asking for any motion on her part.
4. Step away from Fluffy, starting with your right foot. She'll become confused if you step off with your left, since she's been taught to follow your left foot during the heel. Therefore step off with the right foot, giving her the verbal command "stay."
5. As you step away, grab hold of Fluffy's leash with your left hand, raising your hand and arm slightly (but not putting pressure on Fluffy's collar). You may need to practice walking around Fluffy this way, with the leash held in front of her to avoid tangling her with it.

Stay

6. At this point, if you're using hand signals, signal the stay command with your right hand.
7. Repeat steps 1–6 several times, until Fluffy gets the hang of it When she does, lavish praise on her.

THE RELEASE

There are two ways to release Fluffy. The first is to say the word "okay." The second is by giving a follow-through command such as "Fluffy, heel!"

CORRECTING FLUFFY

If Fluffy breaks while in the stay position, revert to the obedience correction described on page 134. Give her three corrections, then repeat the command "stay." And remember, patience is essential when practicing the stay command.

HOW LONG SHOULD FLUFFY STAY?

At the beginning, a reasonable amount of time for Fluffy to stay is one minute. As she masters this command, you can gradually increase the time to three or four minutes. Of course, an eight-week-old puppy's attention span won't be as long as that of a year-old dog's—so use common sense. After all, you know your four-footed best friend best!

DEVELOPING FLUFFY'S CONCENTRATION

While it's terrific for Fluffy to master the stay command in the quiet setting of your home or yard, it's important that Fluffy respond to the command in a real-world setting. In other words, on the street with people, cars, and trucks passing by, or with kids playing baseball in the park.

To accomplish this (assuming Fluffy has demonstrated that she knows what is expected of her), start using simple distractions while practicing the stay command. Roll a ball past her, place her favorite toy near her, have people clap their hands or whistle. Despite these distractions, Fluffy should stay until you release her.

PUTTING THE STAY COMMAND INTO USE

Here is an ideal, practical application for the stay command. A difficult time for many dogs is when people enter or leave the home. If this sounds familiar, you'll really appreciate the stay command!

When Fluffy is at the height of her exuberance, command her to stay as the people enter and situate themselves comfortably in your home. After three or four minutes, release Fluffy by saying "okay." By sitting quietly for this period of time, her enthusiasm should be toned down and her greeting more calm.

DOWN

Now that you have taught Fido to heel, to automatically sit, and to stay in the sitting position, the time has come to teach him to lie down on command—the down command. Prepare yourself for this one! You'll need to take your patience pill, as for some dogs this is one of the most difficult commands to learn.

WHY THE DOWN COMMAND IS SO TOUGH

You're probably thinking, "What's the big deal about teaching Fido to lie down? It's something he does so naturally. It can't be that difficult to teach!" But look at it from Fido's point of view: Lying down is a submissive position. It makes him vulnerable. That's why, until he has the confidence, Fido may fight you on this one.

MASTIFF SEE, MASTIFF DO

It's my belief that a dog should be properly shown what is expected of him prior to your looking for the desired response. In the wild, animals behave both instinctively and from learning experiences directed by their elders. Therefore, correct instruction of the down command hinges upon your ability to properly interact with Fido. In other words, you must show him what you want him to do.

GET DOWN ON YOUR KNEES

I know some of you are saying to yourselves, "Warren's really lost it! There ain't no way I'm going to get down on my knees and dirty myself for my dog!" To those of you, I say please hear me out. In my twenty-plus years of dog training, I've found that the most effective approach to teaching the down is to actually get on your knees, lift Fido's front paws, and place him in the down position.

Yes, the correct teaching of the down command does put some wear and tear on the knee area—but it works! So get into a pair of old jeans, and let's begin.

1. Begin with Fido on your left in the sit position.
2. Kneel alongside Fido.
3. Give him the verbal command to lie down, which is simply "down." Refrain from using the phrase "lie down"—there's no need to complicate matters by throwing in an additional word. You also should refrain from using the word "down" as a correction when Fido is

jumping. It'll confuse him. Reserve the word "down" strictly for when you want Fido to lie down. It should be given in a long, drawn-out manner (similar to the stay command) because we want Fido's attention focused on the word.

4. If you're using hand signals, simultaneously with the verbal command use either hand to give the signal for down. Your arm and fingers should be fully extended in an upright position. Slowly lower your arm forward until your hand is at your side.

5. Repeat the verbal command (and hand signal, if applicable) several times while continuing to kneel at Fido's side.

6. Now place your left arm around Fido's back, gently grasping his left front leg slightly above the pastern (above the paw, below the fetlock) with your left hand.

7. With your left hand still gently grasping Fido's left front leg, do the exact same thing with your right hand on his right front leg.

8. Gradually and gently lift Fido's front end upward (he'll look as if he's begging), then outward, and finally into the down position. While doing this, be sure to keep your thumbs on the insides of Fido's legs. This will eliminate the possibility of his front legs being pushed too close together, causing him discomfort. Also continue to give the verbal command.

9. As soon as Fido lies down, give the stay command. Although he's in the down stay position, it will not hurt to repeat "down, down, down." By doing so, you're explaining the command, letting Fido know exactly what he has accomplished. The quick introduction of the stay command will help reinforce the new down command while building Fido's confidence, since you're using a command he's already familiar with.

10. Finally, don't forget the praise!

Down

WHAT IF FIDO INSISTS ON RAISING
HIS REAR END?

Some dogs have a tendency to raise their hindquarters as their front legs are lifted. This, of course, gives you one dog and one owner in a very awkward position. The best approach to this problem is to straddle your legs over Fido's back, taking care not to place any weight on him. This position will enable you to accomplish step 8 while preventing Fido from raising his rump.

COME

The come command is one of the most important elements of Fluffy's (and your) basic training. It is used to retrieve her when she must be near you.

If Fluffy is a young puppy, odds are she'll stay close to you. However, as time goes on and she begins to feel more independent, her natural curiosity will take over, and she'll begin mischievous investigations in and around your home. This wandering is a perfect time to use the come command to your advantage. You'll be very pleased by the control you'll have.

THE BIG BOO-BOO— USING "COME" AS A CORRECTION

One of the biggest mistakes that an owner can make is to use the come command as a correction. How many times have you seen a dog misbehaving and its owner react by calling the dog to come, then either yelling or hitting the dog when she does? Perhaps you're even guilty of this yourself! By doing this, you're teaching Fluffy to associate "come" with correction. It's only natural for her to avoid or delay her response if correction is implied. It's kind of like when I'd misbehave as a kid and my mother would say, "Just wait till your father comes home. Boy, are you going to get it!" I guarantee I was nowhere to be found when my dad came through that door! It's the same with our four-footed best friends—and I can't blame them. In other words, in order for the come command to be successful, Fluffy should have pleasant associations with the word "come."

TEACHING FLUFFY TO COME

1. Begin by placing Fluffy in a sit position at your heel.
2. Giving the stay command, leave Fluffy and proceed to the end of her six-foot training leash.
3. Call Fluffy to you in an enthusiastic tone: "Fluffy, come!" Since come is a motion command, use Fluffy's name first to grab her attention.

4. Step backward and reel in the leash simultaneously while talking to Fluffy to keep her attention.
5. When Fluffy arrives, give the command to sit.
6. Lavish Fluffy with so much praise that your neighbors consider calling the men in the white coats to take you away! Get down on your hands and knees and play, continually telling Fluffy how wonderful she is for coming when called.
7. Repeat steps 1–6 several times, praising Fluffy *each* and *every* time she comes to you.

STEP SIX CAN MAKE ALL THE DIFFERENCE IN THE WORLD

All seven steps are important. Ignore any one of them and you'll reduce your chance of success by 10 percent. Ignore several of them and the risk factor for noncompliance shoots up proportionately. However, if I had to narrow in on any one step that can really make the big difference, it's step six. Each and every time Fluffy comes to you, don't get lazy. Praise her.

If she believes that each time she comes to you fabulous things will happen, just watch how quickly Fluffy bounds right over. That's the deal you have to make with yourself and with her. You must stop whatever you're doing and fuss over her like nothing she's ever seen before.

WHAT IF FLUFFY DOESN'T COME?

Should Fluffy not respond, correct her with a jerk of her leash. Do not, however, use the word "no," because she may then think that the act of coming is wrong.

There are several things that can sabotage your efforts to teach Fluffy to come:

Come

1. Using Fluffy's name for corrections. Use her name only for positive things.
2. Calling Fluffy for something unpleasant or negative. If you're going to give her medicine, you should go to her.
3. Enforcing the come command inconsistently. You must be in a position to follow through if Fluffy doesn't come. There's nothing worse than letting her know she can pick and choose when she wants to listen to you.
4. Family members running around all day long calling her and then ignoring her if she doesn't respond (or even worse, if she does). Talk to them and explain the importance of consistency in Fluffy's training.

By avoiding the aforementioned mistakes and using lots of patience and praise, you'll have Fluffy coming when called like a pro.

ONCE YOU HAVE FLUFFY
COMING LIKE A PRO . . .

. . . don't assume that you can let her loose and expect the same response. Once she has mastered the six-foot leash, gradually progress to longer lengths of twelve, sixteen, twenty, and fifty feet. Once she's responding properly on the longer leashes, it's time to let her try it off the leash.

COMING OFF THE LEASH

As a rule, I advocate keeping our four-footed best friends on a leash at all times when outdoors. However, there are times that training Fluffy to come when off the leash is important. For instance, let's say Fluffy has jumped over your fence and into the street, or her leash has dropped out of your hand while you're out for a walk in a high-traffic area. Your ability to get Fluffy to come to you when called may mean the difference between life and death or severe injury.

When teaching Fluffy to come while off her leash, try it first in an enclosed area such as a fenced yard. Let her off the leash and call her, remembering to sound (and be) enthusiastic. If you're not getting the proper response, perhaps you should return her to her leash and continue to practice.

"ROPE-A-DOPE" AND OTHER GAMES
THAT CAN TRY YOUR NERVES

Some dogs will do everything in their power to avoid you during their come command lessons. Yet as soon as you stop calling, they come running right over. This is what I call the canine Rope-a-Dope. This situation usually arises when you have played cat and mouse with Fluffy.

Another common situation is when Fluffy comes as you call

but zips away as soon as you reach down for her. Of course, you'll find yourself chasing Fluffy, thereby creating a new game. It's important to remember that in general a dog is more afraid of losing its owner than the owner is of losing the dog. If you kneel down and stay in the same position, Fluffy will usually give up her game and return.

Another major reason why Fluffy might not come as quickly as you desire is that she might not be receiving the proper exercise. A walk three times a day is by no means enough exercise for the average dog. A dog needs to run and will let you know when she's had the needed dosage. Remember, a well-exercised dog is usually better behaved and in better health (see page 198).

Another problem with the come command is the dog that constantly sniffs. Keeping Fluffy's attention at this time is critical. If she's concentrating on you, she won't be as interested in the aromatic amusements around her.

ONCE AGAIN, PATIENCE IS A VIRTUE

It's very understandable if you become frustrated and angry when you let Fluffy loose for a five-minute walk in the country and it takes an hour to retrieve her. Don't vent your anger on her, or the next time she might take two hours to return! Instead, you might want to go back a step and review the come command with her on her leash.

COME FROM MOTION

It's very important that Fluffy respond upon hearing your call. Whether she's chasing a ball, rolling on the beach, or teasing the neighbor's cat, Fluffy must come. If Fluffy is training-wise she may think she has to come only when she's in the sit position. This false notion is corrected by teaching the "come from motion" response as follows:

1. While walking with Fluffy in the heel position on her leash, nonchalantly step back on your right foot and call her to come.
2. Continue stepping backward, calling Fluffy with all the enthusiasm you can muster.
3. When Fluffy arrives, praise her.
4. Repeat steps 1–3 several times.
5. Once Fluffy gets the hang of it, repeat this method using different speeds and paces. In other words, once you and Fluffy have graduated from slow to normal, try it from a fast or running position. This teaches Fluffy to turn toward you when she hears her name.

USING A LONGE LINE

Once Fluffy's mastered the come from motion on her leash, it's time to introduce a new training device—a longe line. Also called a light line, a longe line is a long piece of rope, preferably of a lightweight material.

Take Fluffy to a large, open area and attach the line to her collar. Let Fluffy loose while you hold on to the end of the line. When she reaches the end of the line, call her. If there's no response, give Fluffy a corrective jerk but refrain from saying no. When she responds correctly, give her lots of praise. Again, if you run into problems with this exercise, go back to the basics and build back up gradually.

ONE FINAL PIECE OF ADVICE WHEN TEACHING FLUFFY HER ABC'S

For any of her training to be effective, Fluffy is going to have to respond to the basic commands under all types of situations.

Therefore, during her training sessions she should be exposed to common situations such as children playing ball on the streets, bicycles, cars, other dogs, and menacing cats. It's a good idea to train her in different areas so that she doesn't become accustomed to reacting positively only in the backyard. Take her to a beach, a park, a schoolyard, or anywhere that you might anticipate taking her in the future.

THE MOST COMMONLY
ENCOUNTERED
PROBLEMS

Every week I field hundreds of questions regarding doggy be-havior problems. Some of these are asked on the air by callers to my radio programs on WOR in New York and KABC in Los Angeles. Others come by way of letters to my office or the radio stations. Still others come from people I run into while shopping in the supermarket, dining out, or picking up my dry cleaning. There are a lot of people out there having a lot of problems with their four-footed best friends—problems that can be easily cor-rected!

The number one most frequently encountered problem owners have with their dogs is housebreaking. That's why I've devoted an entire section in this book to it (see pages 96–114). In the following sections I've compiled the other most com-mon problems people have with their canine comrades, plus simple solutions to ensure that you and Fido live happily ever after.

THE SHAKE CAN

Before we start tackling any of these problems, I'd like to introduce you to an indispensible training aide—the shake can. Used as a form of correction for many behavioral problems, the shake can is surprisingly affordable—twenty cents plus the price of a soda! Simply take an empty soda can, fill it with twenty pennies, and tape the top shut.

As its name implies, the shake can is generally shaken in conjunction with saying the word "no" to reinforce the correction. As you will see in the following sections, the noise the shake can generates can be used to correct Fido even when you are not there to do so. Be sure to use the shake can according to the instructions given for the particular problem you want to resolve.

CHEWING

Believe it or not, chewing is a natural behavioral pattern for Fido. From his point of view, chewing serves the same purpose as reading a book, fishing, or lighting a big cigar after dinner. Fido chews to relax. However, dogs chew for many other reasons, and if the behavior is not corrected properly, it can develop into a destructive habit that may threaten your very relationship with Fido.

TEETHING

One reason why Fido chews is because he's teething. Of course, this only occurs when Fido is a puppy. Just as with babies, when a dog's teeth are cutting the gums, there's a lot of pain, and Fido's natural reaction is to chew. If you're lucky, it might just be a sock; however, more often than not, it's some prized possession like your Chippendale chair or your brand new Gucci shoes!

What can you do about it? First, put yourself in puppy Fido's position. He's in pain virtually twenty-four hours a day during the teething period. If your child were teething, you would go to the drugstore and buy a frozen teething ring to soothe his gums. It's no different for puppy Fido. In Fido's case, buy him a dozen natural rawhide bones. If you're a good cook, dip a few of them in a little homemade gravy. If your cooking skills are not up to par, a little low-salt beef bouillon or cheese spread will do. Then place them in the freezer. Keep several of these frozen bones on hand to give Fido when he feels particularly uncomfortable.

You're probably wondering why a dozen natural rawhide bones are necessary. The answer is really quite simple. Just as with children, puppies' attention spans are limited. Thus, puppy Fido will become bored with just one or two toys and—you guessed it—he'll go back to your Chippendale chair or those expensive Gucci shoes. Besides, every piece of natural rawhide has a different taste. So put down five or six bones, leave them out for two days, pick them up, and replace them with five or six new bones. On the fifth day, put away the new batch and replace them with the first batch. By rotating puppy Fido's bones, in essence you're giving him new toys every few days.

Additionally, you'll want to provide puppy Fido with lots of chew toys. In fact, if you're not constantly tripping over them, you're not giving him enough of them! I prefer ones made of latex, since they're more durable. Be careful when it comes to toys that contain squeakers. The squeakers may become loose and be accidentally swallowed. Be sure to check any toy carefully for pieces that could become loose or be bitten off. Use the same common sense you'd use if you were buying a toy for an infant or small child.

And here's a word of encouragement for both you and Fido—teething is usually completed in Fido's eighth or ninth month!

BUT FIDO'S TWO YEARS OLD
AND HE'S STILL CHEWING!

Boredom is perhaps the most overlooked reason Fido chews. When left alone, the bored chewer will chew on anything and, in extreme cases, even on himself. If Fido is a bored chewer, he needs more to do in his life to relieve the boredom. If I were left alone for eight to ten hours every day with nothing to do, I'd start chewing—on food, gum, or even my nails!

To address this problem, put down new or favorite toys just before you leave the house, and pick them up immediately upon arriving home. By doing so Fido's attention will focus on the excitement of these special toys, which are only available when he's alone. Also remember that a bored dog is very often a lonely dog. Leaving the radio on a talk station may combat Fido's loneliness, as human voices can be very reassuring to him. At the very least, you'll have a very knowledgeable dog!

Dogs who are not receiving a nutritionally balanced diet also will sometimes have a strong tendency to chew. In this case the need to chew might be Fido's instinctive search to balance his diet. If your dog chews on or eats plants, dirt, garbage, or even his own stool, have him checked by your vet. He may be experiencing a vitamin or mineral deficiency that all the behavioral correction in the world will not cure.

YOU'RE CONVINCED FIDO'S JUST
BEING SPITEFUL

You don't know how many times I've met owners who insist that their dogs chew out of spite. Maybe you're even nodding your head in agreement. Well folks, don't let this come as a blow to your egos, but no matter how smart you think Fido is, he's simply not capable of plotting to destroy your most valuable possessions just to get even with you for leaving him alone! This so-called spiteful behavior is usually your own fault—created when you overreact to Fido's chewing, thus rewarding him with attention. Even though it's negative attention, in Fido's mind negative attention is better than no attention at all. Think about it. Is the only time you pay attention to your four-footed best friend when you're scolding him? If so, shame on you!

SEPARATION ANXIETY

Another reason you may find your home in a state of destruction every time you return is due to what I call separation anxiety. Especially prevalent in dogs who have had several homes, separation anxiety is truly a psychological problem. Imagine if you were shuttled from one foster home to another or, even worse, abandoned. Then a really nice family takes you in and you really like living with them. They're really nice to you—they play with you and take you on long walks and feed you delicious food. Then your nice family leaves you alone in the house. You're not sure if they're ever coming back—after all, you've been abandoned before! A few minutes go by and no one returns. So you run throughout the house looking for them. You become frantic. You look in the closets and in the pantry, and you wind up knocking things over and making a mess in your frantic search. You become more and more frenzied because you can't find your nice family. In your panic you start chewing on things. It may be Mom's slipper because its scent reminds you of her, or it may even be the moldings around the doors. No matter what it is you're chewing on, the action of chewing soothes you ever so slightly.

When your nice family finally does return, you're so, so happy to see them! Your wag your tail, jump up and down, and run around giving them your biggest welcome. When they see the mess you've made they scold you. They might even hit you, but you don't care because your nice family is back. Sadly, if this scenario is repeated every time the family leaves the house, there's a good chance Fido will wind up back at the pound.

Once you recognize this problem, there are things you can do to remedy it. First and foremost you must reassure Fido that you will return by gradually desensitizing him to your absences. This is accomplished by leaving him alone in the house for brief periods of time. At first, leave the house for five minutes or so. This may mean you leave the house and simply walk around the block. Do this several times during the day. As Fido adjusts, gradually increase the length of time you're away. During your absences, follow the suggestions I've outlined in the section on bored chewers—leave out a special toy, keep the radio playing on a talk station. The point is to build Fido's confidence that you will return. Here, patience is certainly a virtue! This process may take a couple of days or even a couple of weeks, depending on how insecure your four-footed best friend is. Remember, Fido is not being spiteful!

SOLVING THE CHEWING PROBLEM

You don't know how many times I've received the following phone calls to my radio shows: "Warren, Fido keeps chewing on my shoes" and "Warren, Fluffy insists on chewing on my socks." When I ask Fido's owner what she does when she catches him in the act, the usual response is, "I say, 'No!,' take away the shoes, and give Fido a rawhide bone." When I ask Fluffy's owner what he does, the response is usually, "Fluffy has her own sock to chew on. So I take away mine and give her hers."

In both these cases the problem isn't really with the dogs, it's with the owners! Fido thinks, "This is great! Every time I want a bone, all I have to do is chew on a shoe!" And, poor Fluffy, she's totally confused. After all, one minute her owner is giving her a sock to chew on, the next minute she's being reprimanded for chewing on a sock. To Fluffy, a sock is a sock! It's enough to make anyone neurotic!

The point is, it's important to examine your own behavior. Are you sending your four-footed best friend mixed signals? If so, it's time to stop and employ the following methods instead.

First, in order to correct the problem, you can use one of

several products made specifically to deter Fido's chewing. Products such as Bitter Apple and Bitter Lime, which, when used according to their manufacturers' directions, are nontoxic yet leave an unpleasant taste on any items they're applied to. Fido will quickly get the idea that chewing on the rawhide bones you left him is much tastier than chewing on the bitter-tasting chair leg on which you've applied the product. Keep in mind that most of these products contain quickly evaporating alcohol, so it will be necessary to reapply them frequently. Occasionally you'll run into a dog who doesn't mind the taste of the product you're using. In this case, switch to another one. *Never* use products like hot pepper, mustard, or Tabasco sauce. This is not just correction, it's cruelty.

Another good product to use to deter Fido from chewing is alum powder, available at your local drugstore. After clearing its use with your vet, you can mix the powder with a little water to form a paste and apply it to areas where you anticipate Fido will chew. Alum has no odor, but the unpleasant taste will remind him of his deviant behavior. Alum should be replenished every couple of days, as it loses its potency when exposed to the air.

The second, and just as important, step toward solving the chewing problem is exercise. As with many other behavioral problems, lack of exercise can be a major cause of chewing. It is, therefore, crucial to employ exercise as a preventive measure when dealing with a chewing problem. The success of your corrections will be minimal if Fido isn't receiving sufficient exercise. A dog, just as a child, has a certain amount of energy that must be expended. It's up to you to gear this energy into the proper directions.

It's important to keep in mind exactly what type of dog you own. Think about what your dog was originally bred to do. It's absurd to expect a German shepherd, which was bred as a working dog, to be content with three walks a day, particularly as a younger dog. And don't fool yourself into thinking that because Fido spends all day in your big backyard, he's getting enough exercise. Years ago, I had a phone consultation with a client in Texas whose dog was destroying his house with his chewing. When I told my client that his dog wasn't getting enough exercise, my client said that was ridiculous, since the dog had a four-hundred-acre ranch to roam on. I told my client to look outside. Sure enough, there was his dog, lying under a tree just outside the house! The dog needed someone outside with him, playing with him and making him run.

So start with some doggy aerobics or some puppy push-ups (see page 198). Make Fido's backyard an interesting place to play. And don't forget those walks in the park or a Frisbee catch on the beach. The exercise will do you both good!

By being consistent—using the deterrent products on a regular basis, offering Fido chewing options such as rawhide bones and toys, and engaging in a regular exercise routine—your Chippendale chairs, Gucci shoes, and other prized possessions will stay intact.

MOUTHING

"My dog doesn't know how to play. All he does is chew on my hand." You don't know how many times I've heard this dog-owner's lament!

Mouthing is very common among young puppies and sometimes even among older dogs. Puppies will play with their littermates by using their mouths to grab and chew. This is a normal method of play as far as they're concerned, and they may try to continue it with you—their new human playmate! If Fido is between three and six months of age, he may be teething. During the teething period, he'll experience physical discomfort and may become irritable. As a result, he may be additionally inclined to chew on anything in reach—including you!

WHAT NOT TO DO

Never encourage a puppy to play with your hands and arms. It may be cute when he's young, but it can become a painful lifelong habit!

Never overreact to a mouthing problem by hitting Fido or screaming at him. By doing so you're only teaching him a very good way of getting attention—even if it's negative attention. Also, by overcorrecting him with a newspaper or with your hands, you may be encouraging hand shyness and possibly aggressive behavior.

Never assume that because Fido gets three walks a day he's getting enough exercise. This is simply not enough, nor the right type. If Fido is large or a sporting breed, he may be mouthing out of frustration, boredom, and excessive energy.

SOLVING THE MOUTHING PROBLEM

In addition to giving Fido sufficient exercise, you must learn the proper way of correcting him, and do so consistently. If Fido is on his leash and collar, the corrective jerk and no should be used (see page 134). When Fido is not on his leash, incorporate the technique of variable reinforcement while using a firm "no" in conjunction with a good shake of the shake can. Variable reinforcement means that you vary the type of correction you use so Fido never knows what to expect. The element of surprise is crucial, so alternate between using the shake can with a firm "no" and simply the word "no." Do not, however, alternate the corrections in a predictable pattern—the element of surprise must remain intact. Our ultimate goal is to get Fido to respond to the word "no" only—the shake can is used to occasionally reinforce the word during his training.

As after any correction, always give Fido plenty of praise once the mouthing has ceased. Next, offer him a toy or rawhide bone to show him what he should chew. Remember, be consistent.

Do not give up after two or three corrections. Above all, be sure he's getting exercise daily. Even a dog that spends the whole day outside needs to interact and play with you to ensure he's getting sufficient exercise.

STEALING

Is Fido a thief or a kleptomaniac? Does he run off with one of your shoes or the kitchen dishrag or a sock? Does he literally "air your dirty laundry" in front of company, parading through the living room with your underwear in his mouth? Some dogs will steal and chew, and others will just steal. But any way you look at it, Fido is still doing something incorrect with his mouth and should be corrected.

SOLVING THE STEALING PROBLEM

If Fido is a bold thief, it actually makes your correction much easier! In this situation, you'll frequently be able to catch Fido in the act of chewing and stealing, thus making an immediate correction possible. Use the shake can and a stern "no!"

Don't make the mistake of taking the right shoe away from Fido, only to have him then take the left one. You'll need to set up a decoy. By spraying both shoes with Bitter Lime or Bitter Apple, Fido will quickly learn that his toys taste a lot better than your belongings!

But what if Fido steals when you're not home? Again, it's important that he receive an immediate correction. The answer is to bait the counters and tables with his favorite stealing items. For instance, if Fido has a habit of stealing your kitchen dishrag, drape it over the edge of the counter or table—wherever Fido is apt to steal. Then place a shake can on the dishrag. When Fido tries to steal the rag, the can will fall to the ground, making a startling noise. It's like God corrected him!

And believe it or not, balloons may aid in the training of your dog. When blown up, sprayed with one of the deterrent products, and placed in strategic areas, they can be very effective. When they pop, they'll remind Fido immediately that he has done something wrong.

Does Fido "work for the sanitation department" by emptying all the garbage cans in your house? By balancing a shake can on the edge of the trash can and baiting its contents with a bitter-tasting deterrent, you should be able to correct this problem.

HOLE DIGGING

Dogs dig holes for many reasons. Sometimes this behavior is instinctual, as evidenced by the hole-digging behavior of the wolf. During the winter, when food is scarce, a wolf will devour his prey immediately. Yet in the summer, when food is more plentiful, he will dig a hole and bury some of his food, returning at a later date to complete his meal. This is very similar to the dog that buries his bone in one spot in the yard and goes back that evening to enjoy it. Also, a dog left outside in the hot summer months will often dig a hole and crawl into it to be next to the cool earth. In contrast, during the cold winter, the dog may dig for the warmth of the earth under the cold surface.

Now for the problem digger. This is when owner error often comes into play. You see, the dog that doesn't receive enough exercise is a much better candidate for a digging problem. After all, digging is a way for Fido to use his pent-up energy. If Fido doesn't receive enough attention, he may also dig strictly out of boredom. And as with other problems, if you use negative reinforcement—hollering, screaming, a general overreaction—you'll increase the problem. Remember, if Fido is looking for attention, negative attention is better than no attention at all as far as he's concerned.

SOLVING THE HOLE-DIGGING PROBLEM

Now that you know why Fido is digging holes, perhaps you would like to know how to stop it. If Fido is the bold type that digs right in front of you, it's a little easier to correct. Simply use the shake can in conjunction with a firm "no" when you catch him in the act.

If you're the unlucky owner whose dog never digs in front of him, the correction is more difficult but just as effective. Contrary to popular belief, it is not necessary to catch the dog in the act to administer a correction. If you have been out all day and return home to find a hole in your favorite flower bed, use the wooden stake method.

First, stake a piece of wood in the ground in the middle of the hole. Dig a little to freshen up the smell of the dirt. Put Fido on a short leash and tie him to the stake. Leave him attached to the stake for twenty minutes. Come back at ten-minute intervals and shake the shake can while saying "no." At the end of the twenty minutes, untie Fido, but leave the stake in the ground to serve as a reminder to him. After stakes are in several holes, Fido will look at them and associate them with the correction that he received.

I know you'll be thrilled to look out on your yard and see a series of stakes poking out of the soil! While your neighbors might think you're crazy, I assure you that a few stakes in the yard now isn't as bad as a lifetime of hole digging!

JUMPING ON PEOPLE

Imagine living in a world populated by twenty-four-foot-tall giants—a world in which the only way you can make eye contact with these supertall beings is to climb a ladder. The human world is much the same for our four-footed best friends—except, without the luxury of a ladder, jumping is the only way for them to make eye contact.

While Fido (and even you) may see nothing wrong with this type of greeting, other people may not appreciate it. As hard as it might be for you or I to comprehend, not all people are animal lovers. Many are uncomfortable and fearful when around a dog. In fact, many macho men have been brought to their knees! We also mustn't forget that a small child could be knocked down easily or frightened by the exuberant greeting of such a big oaf. Therefore, it's your responsibility to teach Fido that there will be no jumping.

You may be thinking, "But Warren, I look forward to such an enthusiastic greeting from my best buddy when I come home from work!" Don't worry, you can always teach Fido to jump on command. But first, all jumping must be corrected and stopped.

WHAT NOT TO DO

Forget any methods you may have read or heard about that require physical corrections. This means no kneeing Fido in the chest or stepping on his rear paws. Competent trainers and good owners never rely on physical pain. It is inhumane and cruel. Furthermore, from the standpoint of consistency, these corrections are unsuccessful. Such corrective methods must be used each and every time Fido jumps in order to be effective—and I guarantee that not all of your friends who visit you will be willing to apply these cruel techniques. If they are—get yourself a new set of friends!

SOLVING THE JUMPING-ON-PEOPLE PROBLEM

In the ideal correction, you have the control and don't have to depend upon others to follow through with it. That's why the shake can is a great method for correcting jumping. If Fido is jumping on guests when they are coming or going through the front or back door, leave a shake can at each door, both inside and out. You may even want to keep one in your car's glove compartment. By doing so, you'll be completely prepared for Fido's jumping when you return home.

When you begin using the shake can for the jumping correction, your timing must be good. If you wait until Fido is already on top of your guest, you've waited too long. The correction must occur just as Fido is getting ready to jump or is in midair. A firm "no!" should always accompany the shake of the can. Here, again, it's important to incorporate the technique of variable reinforcement. By alternating the form of the correction— using the shake can with a firm "no" sometimes and simply the word "no" at others—you maintain the element of surprise. By occasionally reinforcing the word "no" with the shake can, you will ultimately achieve the goal of teaching Fido to respond to the word "no" only. And remember, just as with Fido's basic training, consistency is extremely important. It's amazing how our dogs remember the one time they got away with something, instead of all the times they were corrected for it!

It's important to remember that most of Fido's behavior problems, including jumping on people, are created by Fido's owners and by the people living with Fido. For instance, when a new puppy is brought into the home, people tend to play roughly with him. This is enjoyable for both parties; however, such behavior teaches bad habits. At a later date this could lead to serious problems. A young puppy frequently is allowed to jump all over people because he's so small and cute. When he reaches five or six months of age and is still jumping all over people, it becomes annoying and dangerous. A forty-pound dog jumping playfully up on a person or child can possibly cause injury. So when the next puppy is brought home, play—but don't allow him to jump.

One of the best ways to correct Fido is through the use of the basic obedience commands we covered earlier. Does the following scenario sound familiar? The doorbell rings. Fido gets very excited, runs to the door, and gets ready to jump on your company as soon as you open the door. You know this is going to happen, so you holler, "One minute. I'll be right there. I just have to put the dog away." By putting Fido away, you're simply avoiding or delaying Fido's jumping behavior, not correcting it! After all, if you put Fido in another room then let him out once your company has been seated in your home, odds are Fido will proceed to jump on them anyway! Finally, in extreme cases, your putting him away may actually cause aggression in Fido. He now associates people with something negative—namely, being locked away.

By using the stay command, you can correct jumping, since generally it will calm him down. Upon hearing your doorbell, command Fido to lie down ("down") and stay ("stay"). Then let your company into the house. In the early stages of his training, use Fido's leash and collar. Their use will enable you to use the corrective jerk and no if Fido requires correction. When Fido ceases to jump, don't forget the praise. Once he's been through this basic training, the problem should resolve itself. If Fido has a tendency to jump as company departs, this same technique can be applied.

FINDING A HAPPY MEDIUM

Some of you who relish Fido jumping on you as part of his greeting or when playing with you may be wondering if you can permit Fido to continue this behavior, yet keep him from jumping at other times. The answer is yes. But first, Fido must understand that indiscriminate jumping will not be tolerated. Then you can follow up with teaching him to jump on command. To accomplish this, no jumping at all should be allowed in the first couple of months. Once Fido's jumping problem has been corrected, then and only then can you start teaching him to jump on command, using the word "up."

JUMPING ON FURNITURE AND OTHER HOUSEHOLD ITEMS

No, you don't have to buy Fido his own couch or recliner! Nor do you have to keep your furniture covered by old sheets or bedspreads. Yes, Fido's jumping on the furniture can be very annoying (and destructive) whether he's a Chihuahua or a Great Dane. There are two basic types of furniture-jumpers—the dog that jumps on furniture when you are present, and the type that waits until you're out of the room.

SOLVING THE JUMPING-ON-FURNITURE PROBLEM

If Fido doesn't hesitate to jump on your newly upholstered chair when you're present, it's most likely a discipline problem. Put him on his leash and collar when company comes, because he's likely to jump on the furniture to be with your guests when they're seated. The leash will enable you to employ a corrective jerk and no if the need arises. When not on his leash, use the shake can to correct Fido.

What if Fido is what I call a sneaky furniture jumper? Take Clydie Poops, for example. Clydie insisted on curling up on his owner's new velvet chair—a chair not even his owner sat in! After correcting him with a series of "no"s, his owner thought the problem was corrected. However, wet noseprints on the chair's velvet cushion told another story!

What do you do when your dog waits until you leave the room to get comfortable? Place shake cans along the edge of the furniture. When Fido jumps on it, the shake cans will fall, creating a noise. Here, again, it's like God corrected him!

LACK OF TABLE MANNERS

Don't be surprised if someday, somehow, when you least expect it, Fido helps himself to the hors d'oeuvres for your party or the roast for that special romantic dinner. You may be unknowingly encouraging this type of behavior by feeding Fido at the dinner table. If you insist on giving him leftovers, wait until after the meal, then give them to him in his own dish, and only in moderation. Sadly, once the problem of Fido begging or eating dinner uninvited surfaces, many people tie him up, lock him in another room, or put him outside, so that the family may eat in peace.

TEACHING FIDO TABLE MANNERS

If Fido steals food, begs, or jumps on someone seated at the dinner table, it's probably due to a lack of discipline. It could also be Fido's way of getting attention—even if that attention is the negative kind. During dinner, give Fido the down-stay command, using his leash and collar if necessary. While Fido's on the leash, use a corrective jerk and no if he attempts to jump at the table. When off the leash, use the shake can and a firm "no." You also might try feeding Fido at the same time that you and your family are eating.

If Fido's shrewd, he may wait until you leave the room before stealing a tasty morsel. If this is the case, line the edges of the table or kitchen counter with paper towels and balance shake cans on them. When Fido jumps up to grab a snack, the cans will fall with a noisy, corrective effect. In severe cases, every time you leave the room, leave a piece of food on the table, but bait it with one of the bitter deterrent products or alum powder. Do so every day or every time Fido is left alone in the kitchen or dining room. As a last resort, you can pretend that you're leaving the room, then hide with a shake can. When you catch Fido in the act, shake the can and give him a firm no. By being consistent and vigilant, you'll be able to have Fido join your family at dinnertime. After all, he is a member of the family!

FEAR OF NOISE

It's heartbreaking to see a little puppy cringing with fear when a motorcycle or big truck passes. It's embarrassing when your trained guard dog cowers during a thunderstorm. Many of our dogs suffer from the fear of noise—mainly due to a lack of exposure or socialization at a young age. It's up to you to prepare your puppy for the noises inherent in the human world and to ease the phobias of your adult dog if he hasn't been properly socialized to such noises.

If you're owned by a dog who is frightened by noise, you know how disruptive his traumatic behavior can be—for both of you. As if his trembling and barking weren't bad enough, you probably have to deal with the dirty looks of your neighbors who have to endure Fido's barking, whining, and howling when a truck backfires or a thunderstorm develops. You also may come home to a house that's been destroyed by his neurotic reaction—chewed furniture, dirtied carpeting, and shredded tissues. It's therefore very important to understand the makeup of your dog and to use those training methods best suited to his personality.

Fido's phobic behavior can take many forms. He may bark aggressively at these noises or become nervous and desperately try to escape under the couch or anyplace where he feels he can seek refuge. He may try to soothe himself by the only form of relaxation he can think of—chewing. If Fido is extremely nervous, he may even vomit or have a severe case of diarrhea. Some owners jump to the conclusion that Fido is simply being spiteful when they return to find their homes in disarray. The truth of the matter may be that Fido was traumatized by noise. If your four-footed best friend occasionally causes such destruction when left alone, think about it. What was the weather like during your absence? Check with your neighbors to see if they heard anything unusual (i.e., firecrackers, a car backfiring) while you were gone. Don't blame Fido for being spiteful—he may have been traumatized by noise, instead.

PREVENTING THE PROBLEM—
SOCIALIZING YOUR PUPPY TO NOISE

If you're the owner of a nervous new puppy, you should work noises into your everyday training program. The best method of noise training is gradually introducing your young puppy to unexpected noise. Puppy Fido might temporarily be surprised if you clap together two pieces of wood, but if it's followed by a great deal of praise and a short play period, he'll become more confident and be less apprehensive the next time he hears this noise.

After he reacts calmly to the noise of the wood, gradually increase the noise level by hitting the wood harder until no visible signs of fear are noticed. He's now ready to graduate to the clanging of pots and pans. Here, again, start at a low level, then gradually progress to a louder level until no reaction is seen. This really isn't as time-consuming as you might think. This exercise could fit easily into your routine. After all, banging pots and pans is easy when you're in the kitchen preparing meals.

By properly exposing puppy Fido at a young age, normal fears that could create a neurotic or psychotic dog may be avoided. You should also incorporate trips to the park, to shopping centers, and to schoolyards into puppy Fido's socialization program. Early socialization will help build a confident, sound temperament.

SOLVING THE FEAR-OF-NOISE
PROBLEM IN THE ADULT DOG

So you're the not-so-proud owner of an eighty-five-pound Doberman that trembles when he hears thunder, and both of you are tired of being the butt of your friends' jokes. Don't fret. This problem can be resolved—and without the use of tranquilizers. While tranquilizers are a quick fix, they mask the problem instead of correcting it. And remember, you may not always be there to administer them when a sudden storm arises.

Begin by turning on your radio—keeping it at a reasonably high volume (without disturbing your neighbors). This constant noise level during a thunderstorm will help drown out the noise, thus calming Fido. If you must be away from home and thunderstorms are predicted, be sure to leave your radio on when you leave the house.

If you're home during a storm, soothe and reassure Fido when he's frightened or divert his attention by playing his favorite game. Don't go overboard with the attention, though. Remember that you won't always be able to be around to soothe him. It's best to act reassuring yet behave as if nothing is wrong. And for heaven's sake don't act anxious—our pets are quick to pick up on our own anxieties!

If Fido is a hard-core nervous dog, use a recording of a thunderstorm to desensitize him. Thunderstorm sound effects records and tapes are available at most larger record stores, or you can record the next storm yourself. Play the thunderstorm at a low volume for Fido. (Okay—you don't have to let your friends and neighbors know you're doing this!) Once Fido shows no reaction to the recording, you may gradually increase its volume. Play it each day at this volume until he shows no visible reaction. Again, increase the volume and follow the same procedure, until you're playing the recording at full volume and Fido is paying absolutely no attention to it. This procedure can be used for any type of noise your dog demonstrates a fear of.

The key to relieving Fido's sensitivity to outside noises is to do it gradually. Don't rush, for if you do, you may seriously traumatize him and create a much worse neurosis. Through patience and consistency you can overcome Fido's anxiety.

THE OTHER NOISE PROBLEM— EXCESSIVE BARKING

Those of you who experience this problem will envy the dilemma one of my listeners to my WOR radio program recently called me about. Her problem was that her dog did not bark! She wanted her four-footed best friend to bark when someone came to the door. Since her dog was not a Basenji (the barkless dog of Africa) and had no physical problems, I advised her to get down on her hands and knees and demonstrate what she wanted her dog to do!

Well, if you're wishing you had such a problem because you're experiencing just the opposite—excessive barking—there is hope!

Barking is the way in which dogs communicate, so when Fido barks, he usually has a reason—even if it's not apparent to us. For example, a dog's sense of hearing is much keener than our own. Very possibly Fido's hearing something strange that we're incapable of hearing. Unfortunately, unlike other problems that cause you discomfort (Fido wetting your favorite rug or chewing on your new shoes), excessive barking will cause discomfort for the entire neighborhood.

A common cause of excessive barking is boredom. In other words, Fido makes noise just to hear himself and keep occupied. It's important to understand why he's bored. Is Fido receiving enough attention when you're with him? Does he get enough exercise to compensate for the time he's left alone? Are you leaving enough toys and bones around the house to keep him occupied? Have you made your yard interesting enough? If you can answer all of these questions with a positive response, then you should have no problem correcting excessive barking.

SOLVING THE EXCESSIVE BARKING PROBLEM

When correcting Fido, always start with the most basic methods, then graduate to the more advanced if they're needed. For example, if Fido barks excessively when you're present, use the leash and collar to correct him. Using the corrective jerk and no will make Fido realize what he's doing wrong. When Fido is off the leash, use the shake can. When Fido is barking, shake the can and say no firmly. You'll need to have plenty of cans ready so that you can repeat the correction as many times as necessary. Remember, consistency is key.

For those of you who are unlucky enough to have a dog that barks only when left alone, leave your radio on a talk station when you leave. This may keep Fido guessing as to whether or not he's really alone. (At the very least, it'll drown out some of his barking!) For the more stubborn dog, tape a typical family conversation one evening, and every ten minutes throw the word "no" into the conversation. This will remind Fido that someone is always there to correct him if he's barking. You'll need a continuously playing tape for this technique to be effective.

Yet another approach is what I call the hide-and-seek method. Pretend you're leaving your home for the day. Since dogs are much more perceptive than we think, be as good an actor or actress as you can. Prior to your departure, make sure you have several shake cans and the juice of a fresh lemon within your reach.

Your biggest performance is about to start! Be sure to follow the same daily patterns. It's important to jiggle your keys at the door as if you were locking it. However, leave your door unlocked for quick entry when Fido's barking begins. If you live in an apartment, head for the elevator and actually push the button to summon it. Your neighbors may not be thrilled with this, but it sure beats listening to Fido bark day in and day out! The point is to make Fido think you have indeed left. If you live in a house, this means actually driving your car out of the driveway and parking it down the block. Quietly walk back to your house or apartment and wait for Fido to start his repertoire. As soon as it begins, enter and show your disapproval. Shake the cans, using an authoritative no at the same time. Then place a drop of lemon juice on Fido's tongue. This will show Fido that what he's doing with his mouth is incorrect. This procedure will have to be repeated five or six times, and probably even more if you have a problem dog. It's time-consuming, but isn't peace and quiet and peace with your neighbors worth it?

Finally, the socialization of your puppy again plays an important role, even with the excessive barker. I was once called in on a one-year-old Lhasa apso that was barking fiercely at everything that went past his apartment door. However, the dog was actually timid and fearful upon meeting strangers. My first question was how much time the dog spent outdoors and in other environments. The answer was almost none. It became clear that this particular dog had no idea of what the real world was like and was therefore barking fearfully at every strange noise. I implemented a crash course in socialization. After two weeks of taking the dog to shopping centers, parks, beaches, and other places, the excessive barking problem simply disappeared. The dog now understood that the outside world did, in fact, contain many noises—both normal and strange. Once he fully understood this, he didn't need to bark at every little sound.

These aren't the only reasons dogs bark, but the method of correction remains the same. You'll have to play detective to determine why your dog is barking, then use the best approach to resolve it. Your neighbors, and your four-footed best friend, will thank you!

AGGRESSION, GROWLING, AND BITING

Aggression is defined as an "outward act of hostility." It has been my experience that hostility in our four-footed best friends generally reflects one or more problems that have been created either by the ignorance of the owners or by their actual abuse. Aggression will usually manifest itself in growling, and sometimes, in extreme cases, in the act of biting. Each particular form that surfaces in a given dog has a cause, hopefully a cure, and almost definitely a prevention.

THE CAUSES OF AGGRESSION

One of the most common reasons Fido acts aggressively is his instinctive desire for dominance. Dogs, being very social animals, will try to be the leader of the pack or, in our case, the family. During obedience training or correction for a particular problem, Fido may challenge you. This challenge means that he's objecting to your superiority. His challenge, which may take the form of barking, mounting, staring, or growling, must be corrected immediately.

If Fido behaves to an extreme in his own backyard, in the house, or under a piece of furniture, he's being territorial or overly protective. As far as Fido's concerned, he's claiming an area, and any intruder is fair game. Along with the overly territorially protective dog is the type that, once obtaining his food, a bone, a toy, or other object, will go to any length to keep it. One dog that I knew had the idea that a rubber ball was to be guarded at all costs. His overly possessive behavior probably had been brought about by a lack of discipline as a puppy. After all, as puppies grow, they test different modes of behavior. If they use a growl to get what they want and succeed, they'll be encouraged to utilize aggressive behavior the next time. Unfortunately, next time the aggression can, and probably will be, more violent. That's why it's so important for you to correct the puppy when aggression first manifests itself.

Speaking about puppies brings to mind yet another point. When puppies are growing, they should be exposed to people. A lack of socialization will cause puppy Fido to fear people, and can be disastrous. Take Tara, a German shepherd who was raised by a family that allowed only immediate family to be near her, and then only to feed her. By the time she was fully grown, Tara would attack any stranger out of fear. And when handled by anyone, she would lose all control of her bowels and mess the area that she occupied. Remember, puppies must be allowed to have sufficient human contact.

The same goes when it comes to exposing Fido to other dogs and animals. Clydie Poops was raised in a strictly human world. While he was exposed to all types of people and seemed well adjusted to strangers, he would bark and lunge uncontrollably at other dogs. His owner was convinced that Clydie thought he was a person and was fearful and threatened by the furry four-footed creatures he met on the street. Clydie's problem stemmed from the fact that he was never exposed to other dogs. His only exposure to them was during his brief walks, and even then his owner would generally cross the street when she saw another dog coming in order to avoid a confrontation. Clydie's lack of socialization to other dogs resulted in him pulling on his leash, standing on his hind legs, and growling and whining at his canine comrade across the street. Clydie's owner only exacerbated the problem by continuing to prevent his interaction with other dogs.

Other owners provoke aggression in their dogs by abusing them—by hitting them with their hands or with objects such as newspapers or broom handles. The dog's reaction will depend on the severity of the abuse. If Fido has been beaten, he'll probably protect himself every time a hand is raised. And can you blame him? This same violent behavior can be brought about by the use of prong collars, electric shock collars, or cattle prods. Each of these items is extremely painful and can create a neurotic biter—so never use them.

Some dogs like to chase objects in motion, such as joggers, bicycle riders, or cars. These dogs do so either from a protective instinct, herding instinct, or an escape complex. We've discussed the first. The second occurs in certain working dogs bred for herding—so keep Fido's breed in mind. This is often a problem with Old English sheepdogs, who nip as their natural herding instincts take over. The third possibility, the escape complex, shows itself in a dog that imagines that you are the prey and he is the predator. As you run away, the dog reacts and goes for the capture in the only way he knows—using his teeth. Obviously, this must be corrected as soon as it is noticed.

Fido may become aggressive out of jealousy, that is, due to a lack of attention that was once his. Fido will often become frustrated—unable to cope without attention. He may vent his frustration on the object he perceives as taking away his attention, whether it is a baby or an adult. I remember a small mixed-breed pup who suddenly started showing aggressive tendencies. When I asked the owners what, if anything, had recently changed in their household, I discovered that their nephew was visiting. Subconsciously, they were ignoring the pup for the boy, which triggered the negative behavior. It's important to follow the steps in the section "What to Expect from Fido When You're Expecting" (page 80) in order to prevent this type of aggression.

WHAT TO LOOK FOR—
THE WARNING SIGNALS OF AGGRESSION

Every owner should be aware of the general physical signs of aggression. Keep in mind that not all dogs will exhibit each and every sign of this violent behavior but all will probably demonstrate certain individual indications of aggression. Being able to recognize these different signs will help you determine the cause of this incorrect behavior.

A dog that is fearfully aggressive will most likely lay back his ears and hold his tail between his legs while demonstrating his aggressiveness. Don't be fooled by the tucked-under tail. Although it's true that the dog is frightened, the possibility of an attack is ever present. He may also crouch and try everything in his power not to make eye contact with you. On the other hand, a dog that is dominantly aggressive, possessive, or territorially aggressive will stand stiffly and erectly, actually measuring taller than what he normally would. His eyes will focus in a direct stare, with his ears and tail most likely held upright.

SOLVING THE AGGRESSION PROBLEM

By being able to read a dog's physical characteristics of aggression, you can determine which type of aggression he is experiencing and what corrective steps should be taken. The fearfully aggressive dog must be corrected, of course, but a bit of compassion and reassurance should also be employed. You should initiate a campaign of socialization and exposure. Until Fido feels confident in different situations and with different people, he won't feel confident in himself, and until he is confident in himself, he will not overcome his fearful aggression. Patience and understanding on your part are key.

Dominant, territorial, or possessive aggressiveness frequently requires a long-range solution. Needless to say, the shake can may be used, but beware: This will sometimes excite a more violent reaction. Exercise your authority by starting a concentrated obedience program. Get out the leash and collar and go through the doggy alphabet. Not only will the obedience training make up for the lack of discipline that has usually preceded this type of aggression, but it also will demonstrate your basic authority. Once your authority has been proven, your dog's challenges gradually will subside. Remember—the going will be slow and rough. Don't expect to see results overnight. Be patient, and by all means don't lose your temper. An aggressive dog will quickly take advantage of your unclear thinking.

Most puppies or adult dogs will show some form of aggression at one time or another. If dealt with properly, it's nothing to be upset about, because it's a normal stage of development. But it shouldn't be left unchecked. Correct aggression the first time it shows itself, and each and every time thereafter.

Finally, if you've followed all the aforementioned suggestions consistently and still have not achieved the desired results, this is the one instance when I advocate introducing a professional trainer.

DOGGY AEROBICS, CANINE CALISTHENICS, AND FIDO'S PHYSICAL FITNESS

EXERCISE ISN'T JUST FOR FAT DOGS

Fido really doesn't need sweat socks or a jogging suit, and he doesn't need to attend an aerobics class with an instructor yelling out "and one and two and three and four." What he does need is his own personal fitness trainer—and you're it. It's up to you to be sure Fido stays on the move long enough to get his heart pumping—at least three times a week. A sedentary lifestyle may very possibly infringe on the quality of his life and his very health and well-being. If he doesn't use it, he loses it.

Any dog—providing the vet says he or she is healthy enough for exercise—should have the opportunities for stretching exercises, to get those muscles limber, and a chance to get some aerobic exercise.

When Fido looks and feels better, he'll better enjoy everything about life—including you. This means more hugging, kissing, and loving will come your way. And you'll be less likely to experience behavior problems with your four-footed best friend. Now what could be better fringe benefits?

OVERWEIGHT DOGS ARE A PRIORITY AND OWNERS NEED TO CLEAN UP THEIR ACTS

"Fido's too fat. I don't understand it." I must hear this from owners a dozen times a week. What's there to understand? I know our dogs are smart, but I have yet to meet one who has learned to plug in the can opener! For the most part, they are not the ones in charge of dispensing food. Only human family members are to blame when Fido's eating habits get out of control (see page 243—"Fido's Diet and Nutrition").

Insufficient exercise and overly sufficient food make for plump poodles, overweight Old English sheepdogs, stout Shih Tzus, corpulent collies, and fat fox terriers. I don't care what diet is on this week's fad list, if Fido's been proclaimed healthy by the vet, there's only one way he can get rid of a tubby tummy—and that's a combination of fewer calories and more activity.

PSYCHOLOGICAL WEAR AND TEAR

Psychologically it's not good for Fluffy to bear the brunt of all those fat jokes. Don't kid yourself into thinking those barbs don't hurt her feelings. Most pets know when you're talking about them, and they can tell by the tone of your voice more or less what you're saying. It hurts Fluffy's feelings when everyone laughs about her stomach leaving trails of its own in the snow. She also knows the joke's on her when she leaps for the couch— and misses.

BIG NUMBERS AND BIG MEDICAL PROBLEMS FOR CORPULENT CANINES

Statistics on the number of overweight dogs vary. However, canine obesity is one of the biggest health problems vets encounter. It's important to keep your dog trim and svelte. Not only will she look and feel better about herself, but the relief from the pressure and stress of extra weight on Fluffy's bones, muscles, and organs could actually keep her from an early grave!

Every owner of every overweight dog I've ever met was loving and caring and would do anything to help his or her four-footed best friend. It's beyond me why these same owners can't make the connection that Fluffy's extra weight could be as injurious to her health as hundreds of other ailments and diseases. Maybe they just don't think it can happen to their dog.

TAKING ACTION

A healthy dog needs to remain active. All the dieting in the world won't help weight loss the way dieting combined with exercise will. Shedding pounds isn't complicated—it just means that Fluffy needs to burn off more calories than she's taking in. Starving her through severe diets isn't right. Having her eat healthy amounts of food and burn off the fat by working out is better.

There are pages and pages of tips throughout this book on how to help Fluffy participate in life rather than simply lie around the house. Encourage doggy activity. Take her for long brisk walks around the neighborhood, build a doggy gym (page 202). Do something. Anything! Just make sure Fluffy gets up and starts moving.

CHECK WITH FLUFFY'S PHYSICIAN FIRST

Before beginning any exercise program, be sure Fluffy has a physical checkup. Tell the vet Fluffy's about ready to start an exercise regimen. Certain age, weight, or medical problems may cause the vet to place limits on or even nix your planned approach to Fluffy's fitness.

START SLOW AND DON'T OVERDO

Don't throw Fluffy headfirst into an exercise program. Don't go for the burn. Begin slowly, then very gradually increase the program every couple of weeks. Please, no crash course for Fluffy. Don't try to make up for lost time—it could make her sick or even kill her! Every dog is a little bit different, so check with the vet for guidelines. A lot depends on Fluffy's present physical condition. Stop before there's heavy panting, and keep your eyes open for signs of too much physical stress, such as a darkening of the pink areas of the inner ears, tongue, gums, and eyes. Deeper pink or red tones could mean Fluffy's overexerted, and you could be doing more harm than good. Also, be alert to a gray color in those same areas. This, too, could be a sign of trouble. When in doubt, stop.

Starting slowly may mean simply taking Fluffy for walks. Over time you can increase the length and pace of these outings. Eventually you may switch over to jogging or a brisk run. If you do opt for jogging, remember that soft, grassy areas are best for Fluffy's delicate pads. Next, you can graduate to covering tougher terrain—hiking on hillier areas as opposed to flat, open areas. The idea is to build up Fluffy's stamina gradually.

Tricks are another good form of exercise. Putting Fluffy through her paces is an ideal form of exercise as long as you make it fun. Don't forget lots of praise! If Fluffy doesn't have any tricks in her repertoire, the basic commands will suffice. For instance, have Fluffy do a series of puppy push-ups by having her go to the down position and back up again.

Or how about doing what one of my clients did? This elderly woman in her eighties kept in shape by dancing. She had me come to her home specifically to teach her papillon to dance with her! Every day they enjoyed sharing a workout—as dancing partners! So go ahead and tap dance with your terrier, marangue with your malamute, or disco with your dachshund!

BUILDING FIDO'S PHYSICAL FITNESS CENTER

Every dog-owning home should have a doggy gym or physical fitness center for Fido. You say you already have a big yard for Fido to play in? What a sport! If all Fido does is lie around in it, it's not doing him any good. You've got to make it interesting so it encourages activity.

No, I'm not suggesting you place a set of weights and an exercise bike in the yard for Fido! There are, however, things you can use to ensure that Fido gets his blood pumping and his heart rate up. Hang an old discarded car tire from a tree in the backyard to serve as a pooch punching bag. Its swinging action will encourage Fido into action. You can also place old tires on the ground for agility exercises. Barrels and old wood skids make terrific exercise equipment—Fido can jump and climb over them. If you have the time and the inclination, you can build hurdles and broad jumps for your four-footed best friend. Of course, take Fido's size into consideration when you build them. If Fido's a pug, don't build him Great Dane–sized hurdles! No matter what Fido's size, don't forget to leave balls and other toys outside for him. The idea is to make your yard as interesting and action-provoking as possible.

WHAT IF FIDO'S AN APARTMENT DWELLER?

Just because you and Fido live in a small apartment in the city doesn't mean that he can't have a physical fitness center. If you can't spare an entire room, set aside a portion of one for him. You'll need to keep this area free of furniture and obstacles. Otherwise, Fido could go skidding into the sofa. Encourage him to play in this area by placing his favorite toys in it. Get down on the floor and play catch with him, using his favorite ball or toy. For your downstairs neighbor's sake, use balls or toys made of fabric or soft, pliable latex—they're quieter.

Take advantage of the stairs in your apartment building. By bypassing the elevator and using the stairs instead, you'll both get an excellent cardiovascular workout. In fact, that's what my friend Lily Tomlin did with her four-footed best friend Tess when they stayed at high-rise hotels while out on the road.

IMPORT A FOUR-FOOTED
PHYSICAL FITNESS TRAINER

If Fido enjoys the company of other dogs, set up regular meetings. It's the easiest way to encourage Fido's fitness. You owners can sit back and have coffee and cake while the pet pals chase around to their hearts' content. Just be sure Fido and his playmates get along well and are up-to-date on all their shots.

DOGGY MASSAGE

If you've ever had one, I'm sure you'll agree nothing beats a good massage. Massage is wonderful and therapeutic for our four-footed friends, too.

Regardless of his age, size, or activity level, Fido can benefit from a massage every once in a while. If Fido is very active, he may suffer from muscle aches and strains, just as we weekend jocks do. A rubdown can ease the discomfort he can't express to you in words. You can tell when Fido is in need of some tender loving care by a certain stiffness in his hind legs or a slower-than-usual response when you tell him to get up after a workout. Bear in mind what I said earlier in this book—be attentive to Fido's body language. A brief massage can work wonders and make that soreness and stiffness vanish.

If Fido is arthritic and/or geriatric, he's a particularly good candidate for massage. The stroking and plying of old or arthritic muscles can really make a difference. This is only partly due to the manual manipulation of muscles and joints. You see, your kind touch lets Fido know that you care about him and recognize his discomfort. For Fido, massage is another form of praise and positive reinforcement—one he'll truly cherish.

GETTING STARTED

No, you don't have to be a licensed Swedish masseur to give Fido a delicious and healthful physical treat! Just be gentle and attentive to your pet's needs. If he flinches or draws away, you're working too hard. The key is to relax and enjoy yourself, and Fido will, too.

Begin by acclimating Fido to being touched. Some animals aren't accustomed to physical contact (shame on you!) and tend to be fearful or skittish when first approached. Certain areas, such as paws and pads, are often very sensitive, and some animals panic when anyone goes near their feet. So before launching into a full-fledged massage, spend a little time each day lightly touching Fido's paws, legs, tail, and any other area he seems cautious about. At the beginning, touch each area for only a second or two and praise Fido profusely. The idea is to gradually increase the amount of time you touch him as you gradually build his trust. Eventually (it may take days or even weeks) Fido will relax enough to enjoy a full-fledged massage.

Fido can be sitting, standing, or lying down for his massage—

whatever position he's most comfortable with. Begin by placing your fingers firmly but gently on his neck and rotating them in a circular pattern. You want your touch to be firm enough to get into his muscles and joints, but not so rough that he complains. Never jerk or pinch.

Keeping your motions steady and your hands always on some part of his body, slowly cover each area thoroughly before you go on to the next. You may hit a spot where muscles are really sore, and Fido may suddenly draw away. This area may be too tight or sensitive to be massaged, so take it easy. Just rub and touch this area gently—try to get the tension to ease up. The massage experience should be relaxing and pleasant for both of you. If it's a struggle, you're doing something wrong—your touch is too firm or you haven't built up Fido's confidence in being touched enough. Simply go back a few steps and take your time.

While the primary massage technique consists of a circular stroking motion, Fido will appreciate a good scratch as part of your massage routine. The scratching of places he generally can't reach—the base of his tail, under his chest, and behind his ears—will be a real treat.

The idea is to massage each part of Fido's body. Give special attention to the areas that are subjected to the most daily physical pressure—his shoulders, back, and hips. He'll appreciate your efforts. Of course, remember that Fido's spine and its vertebrae are fragile, so massage his back with special care. The same goes for the rib cage. And use special care if Fido is small. If you have any doubts about how much pressure you should be using, ask your veterinarian to show you before you get started.

THE IMPORTANCE OF TOUCH

Scientific studies have shown that touch can do amazing things for both humans and animals. It can heal and soothe. It can help lower blood pressure. And it can reassure. When you spend time touching Fido, you're relating to him as another animal does. Massage is a bridge between our language and that of our four-footed friends. It's a nonverbal way of letting Fido know how much you care. Isn't he worth it?

ON THE ROAD
WITH AND WITHOUT
FIDO

TRAVELING WITH FIDO

DON'T LEAVE HOME WITHOUT HIM

Are your well-deserved vacations spoiled because you just can't cope with the anxiety of leaving behind your four-footed best friend? Do you worry so much about Fido's health and welfare that it's difficult to relax and have a good time? Or do you avoid going on vacations simply because you know you'll miss the comfort of his furry body curled up next to yours at bedtime?

When it comes to vacation time, many dog owners make excuses to friends and family as to why they can't go away. They're afraid of becoming the target of ridicule for allowing dogs to rule their lives. If friends and relatives have you thinking that there may be something wrong, that your attachment to Fido is unnatural—well, just quit thinking that! You're not alone. A lot of caring canine owners feel exactly the same way. Their dogs are members of the family, and they would no sooner take a family vacation without their dogs than one without their children. Plenty of dog owners would love to pack up their four-footed best friends and take them on a holiday, but they're afraid of the unknown, envisioning a frenzied Fido, totally stressed-out from the journey and from being in a strange, new environment.

The other option (unless you're lucky enough to have a friend who just loves to take care of your dog, and a dog who just loves being taken care of by your friend) is to leave Fido with the vet or at a kennel. However, for many of us, the choice of steel cages, barking dogs, yowling cats, and care provided by strangers is not a viable solution—no matter how professional and perfect the boarding facility may be.

THE SOLUTION

Well, you don't have to leave home without him! You can take Fido on your trip as long as you make special arrangements for your four-footed vacationer. Since it tends to be hectic just before a trip—there are always a million and one things to do before you leave—make a checklist or refer to this chapter when vacation time rolls around. You don't want to get caught short, especially when it comes to caring for someone who's so dependent upon your organizational skills.

SAFEGUARD YOUR DOG'S
HEALTH AND WELFARE

Arrange for Fido to have a medical checkup before the trip. While you're at the vet's, get a health certificate stating that Fido has been known to the vet for a number of years (if that's the case), is in good health, and is up-to-date on his vaccinations. Inquire with the state, country, or your transportation carrier as to how close to the time of travel the pet must be examined (a good travel agent will also be able to give you this information). A health certificate from six months ago will not be sufficient. Fido will need a recent health certificate when crossing borders into other countries, and should have one prior to airline travel even on domestic flights (although they often fail to ask to see it at check-in time).

Be sure to have your veterinarian's phone number with you. Also, bring along any prescription drugs Fido's required to take and an extra prescription that can be filled, or at least referred to, by a vet licensed to practice in your vacation area.

TWO FORMS OF ID, PLEASE

For underaged kids trying to sneak into bars, the most dreaded words in the world are "two forms of ID, please." The policy of requiring two forms of ID may prevent youngsters from abusing alcohol, and it can help safeguard Fido, too. While traveling, things tend to fall off or break, so be equipped with some extra doggy ID—one tag for the collar and another packed away to replace the original if necessary. Include your phone number as well as that of your vet or someone else you can count on. Remember, you and your family will be out of town, so if Fido gets lost, no one will be at home to answer the phone.

While you're doubling up on equipment, toss in an extra collar and leash.

HUSH-A-BYE AND SWEET DREAMS

If you want your four-footed best friend to quickly settle into his new space, be sure to pack either his bed, favorite pillow, security blanket, or special towel. Even if your dog can fall asleep anywhere, anytime, having his special blanket along will add to his sense of well-being.

HAVE TOYS, WILL TRAVEL

It's equally important to pack some of Fido's toys. Playing with a few old favorite items may be just the trick to maintain Fido's sense of security while he adjusts to a new environment. Pack a few new ones, too. When you break out all these goodies, he'll associate his vacation home with having a great time.

WHERE WILL FIDO SLEEP?

More important, where will his owners sleep? Don't be afraid that you won't have anywhere to stay if you bring Fido along. It's up to the management of each hotel within most chains to set the pet policy, and a percentage of them do allow dogs. If you run out of luck with the major hotels, try bed-and-breakfast hotels (or should that be bed-and-whiskers hotels?). Sometimes their policies are more flexible. There are even several publications available that list pet-friendly accommodations by location. In any case, call ahead and, if necessary, offer to sign an agreement holding you responsible for any damage Fido might do. You might also offer to forward an additional security deposit. You and I know that Fido is a perfect gentleman because you've applied the techniques in this book, but the hotel manager hasn't met Fido yet!

When you check out after a successful stay, try to get a letter from the management describing your dog's good behavior. If you manage to collect a few letters over the years, it will certainly help ease your way into hotels that have stricter pet policies.

Several years ago, my wife and I took Tige with us on a trip down South. Our travels took us to the state of North Carolina, which at that time had a state-wide policy of not allowing pets at hotels and motels. Knowing of this, but needing a place to spend the night, I wrapped Tige in a blanket and held him in my arms like a baby. As we registered at the front desk, my wife couldn't contain her laughter—Tige's tail was sticking out of the blanket and was wagging up a storm! Lucky for us, the hotel manager had a sense of humor. He said that anyone who went through so much trouble to disguise a dog in order to smuggle him into a hotel deserved to stay. I do not, however, recommend you try this tactic—the management may not be as tolerant and understanding. It's always best to call ahead and get permission.

After you've arrived at the hotel, even if you're tired, take your dog's carrier to the room yourself. A ride on the bellhop's cart can be a little bumpier than Fido likes.

It's not a good idea to leave your dog alone in the hotel room (some hotels don't even allow it). If you must, call the front desk and alert housekeeping. Notify everyone not to come into the room, and hang the DO NOT DISTURB sign on the door. Besides petnapping, the big concern is that someone entering the room will allow Fido to run out the door. You might consider leaving Fido secured in the carrier, or blocking the area around the door. This way, if someone should walk in, Fido won't bolt out of the room.

A DOGGY BAG FOR FIDO'S FIRST AID

Packing a first-aid kit for our canine kids is a must! Dogs in new environments, just like children, tend to be curious, and their instincts to explore might get them into trouble. They're more apt to check out foreign objects, so be sure to read about the Heimlich maneuver (page 254). There's also a strong possibility of an upset stomach or other illness occurring due to the stress of traveling, change in water, etc. Remember: First aid is only an immediate, temporary, emergency measure, a stopgap until a veterinarian can be consulted.

For Fido's first-aid kit, take along:

• Gauze.

• Bandages.

- Diarrhea and stomach-upset preparations. Include a note giving the vet's recommended dose.

- Unbreakable rectal thermometer (normal temperature is approximately 101.5 plus or minus 1 degree, depending on the individual dog, time of day, and recent activity level).

- Petroleum jelly for easier thermometer insertion.

- Insect-bite stick.

- Flea and tick products.

- Wound disinfectant.

- Scissors.

- Tweezers.

HELP AVOID TUMMY UPSETS

A change of diet, water, and environment certainly increases the risk of Fido having a sensitive stomach. To help avoid doggy upset tummies (and your doing the type of cleaning up you didn't envision doing during your supposedly relaxing vacation), bring enough water from home for the entire trip. If your trip will be a lengthy one and you can't see yourself hauling a tanker truck with you, at least bring along a sufficient supply to gradually wean Fido onto the new available water. Also, check to see that Fido's usual brand of food is available at your destination as well as at any stops along the way. If it is not, pack up as much of it as possible. If you're leaving the country, you'll want to check with customs officials as to whether you can bring Fido's food and water with you.

TAKE CARE OF BOTH ENDS

Don't forget about the necessary equipment for Fluffy's mouth and tush. If her food dishes at home are unbreakable (which they should be), bring them along. A lightweight alternative for a smaller dog is a couple of clean pound-size margarine containers. If Fluffy eats canned food, remember to take a can opener. Almost everyone forgets this little appliance.

As the saying goes, "What goes in must come out." The same holds true for Fluffy. If your four-footed best friend is accustomed to relieving herself on newspaper or paper towels—this is particularly common with urban dogs whose communities have so-called pooper-scooper laws—be sure you have some on hand. If your dog is one of a small but growing group of dogs that is litter-box trained, pack Fluffy's litter box and favorite liner. If she's not fussy, many pet stores are now carrying portable folding cardboard litter boxes. They work and they're easy to carry. Be sure to check on the availability of Fluffy's litter box liner at your destination.

SHOULD FIDO HAVE HIS OWN SUITCASE?

By now you're probably thinking that Fido needs his own suitcase for all the stuff I'm suggesting you take along. Or maybe you're wondering whether it's worth bringing him along with you on your travels. Of course it is! You wouldn't leave your kids at home on a family vacation. Didn't you pack bottles, formula, diapers, toys, and baby aspirin for your kids when they were little? Your dog is a living, breathing member of your family and deserves the same consideration.

TO FEED OR NOT TO FEED,
THAT IS THE BIG QUESTION

Common advice on whether to feed Fluffy prior to travel recommends no food for up to six to twelve hours beforehand. Personally, I don't follow that advice unless I find that a particular dog does best that way. Although I cut back on the food intake ahead of time in order to avoid risking a queasy full stomach or making Fluffy uncomfortable because she needs to eliminate, I find that most dogs do well when they have a bland snack before traveling. A snack seems to help absorb stomach acid that might otherwise sour Fluffy's already stressed travel tummy.

Leaving water in Fluffy's carrier is another consideration. While it's nice for her to have drinking water at her disposal, nine out of ten times the water spills during transport. The result is often one very soggy doggy. There are waterers available that only dispense water when licked. If your four-footed best friend gets the hang of using one (you might try smearing some of her favorite food on it to encourage her to lick it), let her travel with it.

PREVENTING CAR CHAOS

Car travel requires dogs to be willing passengers within the confines of an automobile. Before embarking on a long trip, be sure Fido feels comfortable being in the car. Later in this chapter I'll give you some tips to help ensure a happy trip for all your family members.

CAN FLUFFY FLY?

I've resisted adding any number of terrible jokes about flying dogs. With that said, the answer is yes, dogs can fly, by plane. Unfortunately, unless she's a tiny breed that is permitted to travel with you in the cabin, Fluffy will probably have to experience the less glamorous cargo section.

Regardless of what section of the plane Fluffy will be traveling in, be sure that she's adjusted to a dog carrier that's approved for airline travel (see page 226). On the carrier, put a label with your phone number and emergency phone number both on the outside and the inside, just in case the outer label rips off. And be sure your precious cargo is labeled as well. Should Fluffy somehow escape from her carrier, ID tags attached to her collar will facilitate her reunion with you. Speaking of collars, Fluffy should never travel wearing a choke-chain or slip collar. You know how I feel about these types of collars to begin with (see page 119). If such a collar were to catch on the inside of the carrier, the results would be tragic. Instead, use a leather or nylon roll-type collar that fits comfortably. Also, never tie a leash or rope around the carrier or use an ID label that ties on to the carrier. If it fell inside, Fluffy could become entangled in it and choke to death.

Line the bottom of the carrier with something soft and absorbent. Try biodegradable disposable diapers if you're positive Fluffy won't attempt to eat them. Pack extra carrier lining material in your carry-on luggage. If Fluffy has a potty accident while you're around (either while waiting to be placed in the cargo section, or during the flight if she's lucky enough to be in the cabin with you), you can quickly and discreetly change the carrier lining. Even if a potty mishap occurs while Fluffy is in the cargo section, at least the urine will settle into the lining, keeping her comfy and eliminating some of the odor.

Finally, place Fluffy's favorite blanket or towel in the carrier to make it feel a little more like home. You say that she doesn't have a favorite blanket? Then try using an unwashed article of your clothing. No, I haven't lost it! By placing something soft that contains your scent in the carrier—such as your towel, T-shirt, or even a pillow case—Fluffy's travel environment will seem a little less foreign to her.

BOOKING THE RIGHT FLIGHT FOR FLUFFY

Make reservations well in advance, and let the reservations agent know that you're traveling with your four-footed best friend. You'll find that some airlines are more lenient and accommodating when it comes to transporting our pets than others. As a general rule, unless Fluffy is tiny enough to fit in a carrier that can be placed under your seat, she'll be required to fly in the pressurized cargo area. Be sure to check around, because even under-seat measurements vary from airline to airline.

Always book a direct flight if Fluffy isn't traveling with you in the cabin. While most people prefer nonstop flights themselves, it's virtually a must for her. With stopovers and plane changes there are greater risks of human error. We've all heard stories about disappearing luggage. What if that were Fluffy?

Keep temperatures in mind when scheduling landing and departure times, particularly if Fluffy is traveling in cargo. When traveling to a hot climate, schedule your departure and arrival for the cooler times of early morning or late evening. This will help reduce the risk of harm to a dog who's been accidentally left in a hot area during loading or unloading, or—heaven forbid—who's trapped if the carrier gets lost. Of course, do the opposite when traveling to cold climates—schedule your traveling during the warmer times of day.

WATCH OUT FOR THOSE QUARANTINE LAWS

Always inquire about a country's quarantine laws—some countries have them and some countries don't. In 1989, Liza Minnelli unknowingly ran afoul of Swedish law for not observing animal quarantine requirements.

Sometimes even different areas of the same country have variations on the quarantine law. For instance, in the United States, Hawaii has a multimonth quarantine for pets coming in from the other states as well as from foreign countries.

A "TIP" IN CASE FLUFFY HAS TO FLY
IN THE CARGO SECTION

If you must send your dog via the pressurized cargo area (which I don't recommend unless it absolutely can't be avoided), don't be cheap. Tip, tip, and tip again any airline personnel who might be handling the dog carrier containing your precious cargo.

Wait until the last possible minute to send Fluffy off to the baggage area. You might be told over the phone that she has to be loaded one or more hours before departure. While you certainly should arrive by the appointed time, once you're at the counter, animal-loving airline personnel will often let you wait until the last twenty minutes before saying good-bye to her.

TRAVELING ON
TRAINS AND BUSES

Fido may not be welcome on trains and buses. Check ahead of time. Some countries' regulations are more accommodating than others. The United States is tough, but France is fairly flexible. If Fido is able to ride the rails or bus, be sure to follow all the same safety steps as with other forms of travel.

ONE DOG OR TWO?

If you're traveling with two tiny dogs, you might be tempted to squeeze them both into one carrier. Don't do it, even in a large carrier. Apart from some airlines not allowing it, it can make traveling more difficult. I don't care what great buddies they are or that they're so insecure they need each other's companionship, it may be very hard for them to tolerate such close confinement while traveling. You may find that tight quarters are enough to fray their nerves and cause nasty behavior. If you've traveled by car with the kids on a particularly long ride with no rest stops, you probably know exactly what I mean!

TRANQUILIZERS

SHOULD FLUFFY
HAVE HER OWN PILLBOX?

Dog tranquilizers are a hot subject of debate. I don't use them with my dogs. I prefer to take the lengthier route of ensuring my dogs are well adjusted to the rigors of travel. Tranquilized dogs must deal with both the stress of the trip and unnatural drugged feelings that can't be explained to them. Some even suffer side effects.

Although I've never owned a pet who couldn't adjust to travel without tranquilizers, I can appreciate that some dogs (and owners) simply can't get the hang of traveling without them. So if you think Fluffy needs to be chemically lulled into traveling, ask your vet for a prescription and follow his or her instructions very carefully.

PSYCHOLOGICALLY DESENSITIZE FIDO

SPECIAL TIPS FOR FRIGHTENED FIDO
AND FIRST-TIME TRAVELERS

If Fido's never traveled before, or if you suspect he may be frightened, there are some extra steps to take to make his adjustment to traveling smoother. Try them as an alternative to tranquilizers.

If Fido's going to be a jet-set pet for the first time or you know he's nervous about flying, take him to the airport before the trip. This will give him a chance to get used to the hustle and bustle. It will help his sensitive ears adjust to the noise of people and planes and allow his nose to adjust to the foreign odor of jet fuel.

If extra trips to the airport are simply out of the question, at least get a sound-effects recording of crowd noises and planes taking off and landing. Play the recording at a low volume at first. As Fido becomes accustomed to the volume over a period of weeks, gradually increase the level. The same can be done as a preparation for car travel by purchasing a recording of automobile and truck noises.

ONCE YOU'VE ARRIVED
AT YOUR DESTINATION

POTTY ETIQUETTE

Even if your hotel or motel permits pets, it's still best to walk Fluffy away from the hotel grounds. Always scoop up the poop.

If your dog is paper-trained or is one of the few who uses a litter box, be extra meticulous about cleanliness. While you may be desensitized to that little extra doggy odor, others may not. If the papers or litter can't be flushed down the toilet, don't just dump it in the pail in the room and have someone else get stuck cleaning it up. I know you're on vacation, but that's what gives traveling pets a bad name. Instead, wrap it up well and ask management for the location of the outside Dumpster. We shouldn't expect others to do our dogs' dirty work!

AHOY, SEA DOG!

If boating is on your itinerary, be sure to purchase a life preserver made especially for dogs. Yes, they really do make them, although you'll probably have to track one down at a pet specialty or novelty store. Adjust Fido to the life preserver well in advance. (Read pages 121–123 again, and follow the directions, substituting the preserver for the leash.)

When Fido's on a boat, be sure he has access to a shaded area, is restrained with a leash, and is supervised at all times. Do not take anything for granted when it comes to the safety of your dog.

If fishing is on your agenda, remember that fishhooks hurt a lot when lodged in delicate paws and skin. It may not even be your fault; the temptation of something shiny and wiggly at the end of your fishing line might be more than Fido can resist investigating. In a flash, Fido could leap and *ouch*—there's going to be a big problem.

Soda pop, beer, and juice are great thirst quenchers for us, but not for Fido. So be sure to bring along a doggy thermos filled with cool water.

Keep in mind all the precautions in this section if your leisure time will be spent around a pool or lake, at the beach, or just near the docks. Also keep in mind that hot sand can hurt tender feet, particularly of those dogs accustomed to life on padded carpeting.

EVERYONE INTO THE POOL
(OR OCEAN, OR LAKE)

If Fido wants to join you for a refreshing dip, the same rules and warnings apply to him as to any child. Never let him go into the water unsupervised. Even if he's a good swimmer, be wary of the dangerous undertow of the ocean and the strong currents of rivers and streams. Keep an eye out for litter on the beach or along the banks of rivers and streams—we don't want any cut paws. In rural areas, watch out for snakes and other potentially harmful aquatic inhabitants. And of course, be sure the water is clean. If you wouldn't venture into it, don't let your best friend, either.

Speaking of water quality, be sure to rinse Fido with fresh water after he's taken a dip in the pool. The chlorine can be as drying and irritating to his eyes, skin, and hair as it is to yours.

Finally, if you're at a public beach or hotel pool, check to see what their regulations are regarding pets, and abide by them.

IS EVERYONE READY TO GO?

I have a friend who is confronted with the same situation whenever she prepares to go on vacation. As soon as she gets out her suitcase, Bergen—the Great Dane who owns her—starts to mope. Bergen sadly follows my friend from room to room as she packs for her trip. From the moment Bergen sees the suitcases, she never lets her mistress out of her sight. The guilt trip Bergen puts my friend through is nearly enough to make my friend cancel her vacations!

So when you're packing and discover your four-footed best friend is sitting in your suitcase with upset, soulful eyes, remember—you don't have to leave home without him!

HAPPY CANINE CAR TRAVEL

ADJUSTING FLUFFY TO THE CAR
AND COPING WITH CAR SICKNESS

Hooray! No more whining dogs. No more jumping from front seat to back seat and back again. And no more carsick canines. Fluffy can be taught to ride in an automobile like the well-mannered dog you know she is. She can be taught not only to tolerate car travel but to actually love it. You may not believe it now, but the time will come when Fluffy will actually look forward to your rides together.

THE BIG MISTAKE

Don't fall into the trap of putting Fluffy in the car only when she needs to go to the vet's office. How would you feel if the only time you rode in a car was to go to the doctor to have your body probed and to receive a shot with a big, long needle? I know you'd have to drag me into the car kicking and screaming!

For a lot of dogs, their only experience with cars is negative and associated with stress—the stress of going to the vet's or maybe to the kennel. How can we possibly expect our four-footed best friends to know the difference when we decide to take them on the occasional car trip? When Fluffy sees the car, as far as she's concerned, it's doctor time again. She's smart enough to put two and two together, and she says, "Forget it. Thanks but no thanks, I'm heading under the bed. Just try to get me out of here."

If you begin training your dog to enjoy car travel and not just to use the car as a means of getting to the vet's office, you'll be able to plan some terrific vacations that include your canine comrade. And if you find yourself in an emergency situation and have to take your four-footed best friend in the car for an extended length of time, you'll be prepared. Let me tell you about something that happened to Tige and me.

TIGE'S MAJOR CAR EXPERIENCE

I gained a whole new respect for Tige when, due to circumstances beyond my control, I thrust him and his kitty brother, Mowdy, into a traveling situation that warranted giving them medals for excellence. I was expected to be in Orlando, Florida, to appear on a television show at Disney/MGM studios in Disney World. It was a brand-new facility then (the official grand opening hadn't even taken place), and it was the first week of taping for *The New Mickey Mouse Club*. I was the club's "creature keeper" and was doing a segment with a stageful of dalmatians— sort of a takeoff of the Disney movie *101 Dalmatians*. The taping was on Wednesday, and I had tickets for a Tuesday flight. On Monday, New York suffered a major snowstorm, which meant major delays at the airports. On top of that, a pilots' strike was in effect at one of the airlines, and there was some talk that pilots from other carriers were going to honor the picket lines. Being a baby boomer who grew up with *The Mickey Mouse Club,* there was no way I was going to miss that taping. Being a part of *The New Mickey Mouse Club* was my little piece of television history. Besides, there were all those dalmatians waiting for my arrival! So, at nine o'clock Monday night, I loaded up the dog, the cat, and my wife (not necessarily in that order), got into my four-wheel-drive truck, and off we went—slowly. The snow and subsequent ice storm lasted all the way through Virginia. I figured we'd have to drive through the night, but also that we'd get to Florida in time to relax in the late afternoon and get a really good night's sleep. No such luck. Because of the storm it took nine hours to travel the first three hundred miles. My little four-footed passengers, Tige and Mowdy, took it in stride.

Then, somewhere around Savannah, Georgia, I got a tooth-ache the likes of which I had never felt before. Even though I was crazy with pain, I decided to tough it out myself. Tige and Mowdy weren't sure what my bizarre behavior was all about, but those two little angels knew something was wrong, so they sat ever so quietly, not even asking to go for a walk.

We were in the middle of I-don't-know-where, Georgia. The next big city was Jacksonville, Florida. At this point I was screaming with pain. At ten o'clock Tuesday night—twenty-five hours after we started—we located a dentist willing to see some stranger off the street. Tige and his brother continued to behave like angels. Well, I got all shot up with Novocain and got a couple of prescriptions to help me through the next few days. Luckily we found an all-night pharmacy. My four-footed passengers were still behaving as good as gold. Off we continued to Orlando, which, unbeknownst to me, was still three hours away.

We finally rolled into Orlando at three A.M.—a full thirty hours after we left New York. We had to be at the television studio at seven in the morning, so, after only three hours' sleep, I got up, packed up Tige and Mowdy one more time, and went to the studio. Those two darlings stayed, with the exception of a few walks, in the dressing room all day. We didn't finish until six o'clock that night. Through it all, Tige and Mowdy didn't miss a beat—no accidents and no whimpering or crying. I would have understood if they had never spoken to me again. But, of course, they did understand and didn't hold a grudge. What can I say about my little furry friends? They're great. We had a family experience we can all look back on and laugh about. But if it wasn't for Tige and Mowdy's car-riding skills, things could have been a lot worse.

TAKING FLUFFY ON VACATION

I know what you're thinking, "Great story, Warren, but Tige and Mowdy are your pets and were perfectly trained by you. There's no way I can hope to do the same with mine."

Granted, even dogs that do well on a five-minute ride to the beach may have an entirely different opinion of a five-hour ride to vacationland. Few dogs would tolerate what Tige went through. In psychological lingo, it's called flooding—throwing too much at our canines all at once. The solution is to build up to it slowly. Even dogs who are car lovers may need some training for longer rides. But it can be done.

FLUFFY NEEDS TO BUCKLE UP

Before Fluffy goes for any car ride, her safety and the safety of other passengers must be considered. Fluffy should be restrained in one form or another. A restraining device serves two purposes. If, heaven forbid, there's an accident or even an abrupt stop, Fluffy could be thrown about or even out of the car like a rag doll. Even if she survives the impact, her fright might cause her to run off, never to be seen again. Or worse, she might run into the path of other vehicles. Second, it is equally important to prevent Fluffy from interfering with the driver in any way or from working her way onto the floor, where she might become wedged in around the gas and brake pedals. I know of more than one accident that occurred while a frantic driver tried to untangle a dog from the floorboard pedals.

RIDING ON THE BED OF A PICKUP TRUCK— AN ACCIDENT JUST WAITING TO HAPPEN

Time and again I see owners of pickup trucks and other open-bed vehicles allowing their dogs to ride unrestrained in the back. All it takes is one short stop or collision for a tragedy to happen. The driver may walk away unscathed because he was sitting in the protected steel-reinforced cab of the vehicle. The dog may not be that lucky. Additionally, I don't care how well-behaved you think your dog is. If he's riding unrestrained and happens to see another dog or animal along the road, there's no guarantee that he's not going to jump out of the vehicle and into traffic.

FIRST, THERE'S A DECISION TO MAKE

When choosing a restraining device, there are several options to consider. Some owners like it if Fido rides in a dog carrier. Others don't like the confinement of a carrier, choosing instead to educate Fido to sit still in a doggy seat belt (yes, they really do make them. Would I kid you?). Still others prefer to have a passenger hold Fido on a leash.

If you decide on the leash or a seat belt, read the information on pages 121–123 again. (The advice for acclimating Fido to a leash can also be followed for a seat belt.) If a seat belt is your choice, you might be able to find one at a pet shop that carries novelty and specialty items.

SELECTING A CARRIER

What to do, what to do? It's so confusing. There are so many types of dog carriers on the market. Most people don't have a clue as to which one to choose and are often misled by salespeople who may or may not have the appropriate knowledge to make such purchase suggestions. Much of your decision should be based on the nature of your travel needs. There are pros and cons for almost any selection. Final approval, however, rests with Fido. If he doesn't like it, everyone's stuck.

THINK AHEAD

When you're plunking down your hard-earned money on a carrier, buy one that fits all your possible needs, not just the car travel you have in mind today but the air travel that might take place in Fido's future. Buy the right carrier now and you won't have to buy or rent another one later. So my first suggestion is to buy a carrier that's suitable for car travel and is also approved for use by the airlines. The ones I like best are made of molded plastic and are fairly standard. If you're owned by one of the tinier breeds, be sure the carrier is designed to fit under an airplane seat. Airlines vary in their size restrictions for dog carriers, so be sure your choice meets the standards for most of them.

WHEN OTHER CARRIERS WILL DO JUST FINE

If your fear of flying precludes any possibility of Fido entering the world of jet-setters, then there are other types of carriers that will serve the needs of car travel. Make sure the carrier is sturdy. Be a good consumer—check around the seams and locks, and for rough edges that could harm Fido. Test the effectiveness of the locking system. Also check the handle or carrying strap. Has it been attached with double stitching or an extra set of grommets for added strength? Are there sufficient openings to allow good ventilation? Although wicker types are attractive, I'm always fearful they will come apart when I least expect it. If Fido is tiny enough, you might prefer a shoulder bag that he just pops into. Be sure it has enough support on the bottom and enough to hold up the sides. Insufficient support can cause Fido to get all scrunched up while riding along on your shoulder, and when the bag is placed on the floor the unsupported sides will just cave in around him.

Some dogs love carriers with clear plastic tops; some dogs are nosy and won't be happy unless they can see everything that's going on around them. For shy or less secure dogs, this is frightening—any carrier allowing them to see too much passing scenery is psychologically overwhelming. Also, clear plastic tops offer no protection from the sun. Even the winter sun beating down on Fido through the car windows can be too hot.

Check out a variety of different carriers before you make a choice, but do rule out the cardboard versions. They don't offer nearly the security I demand when traveling with such precious canine cargo.

ENSURING A GOOD FIT— HOW BIG IS BIG AND HOW BIG IS TOO BIG?

The rule of thumb is that Fluffy should have enough room for the length of her body and then some, as well as for her height, again with a little to spare. Fluffy must be able to get up and turn around in order to get comfortable. But don't be fooled into trying to be kind by providing an extra-large carrier for Fluffy's trip. Too much extra space inside the carrier means Fluffy will be thrown about as she slips and slides during her transport.

GETTING FLUFFY COMFY IN THE CARRIER

Visions of getting Fluffy into a carrier sometimes resemble really bad nightmares. There's Fluffy whining away with all four paws pushing out in different directions as you try to wrestle her into the carrier's opening. You're hoping that once you get her in she won't pop out before you have a chance to close the door. You're also hoping all of this gets done with no blood shed— hers or yours. Of course, if Fluffy's clever or has been through this before, she'll take one look at the carrier and—adiós, she's out of there, speeding into her favorite hiding place in record-setting time. I'm sure a lot of you are familiar with this scenario. But it doesn't have to be that way.

The key to Fluffy's successful introduction to her carrier is time and patience. Don't just dump the carrier on Fluffy all at once. Take it one step at a time. Place the open carrier in an area where she spends a lot of time. Place something soft and comfy on the bottom so she's not forced to lie on a hard, cool surface. Her favorite blanket or towel would do just fine. Put some of her favorite toys and treats in there, too. Then leave things alone. Don't bring her over to the carrier and don't react to it. Just leave it on the floor for a week or two (or longer for dogs who are really frightened of carriers) until you see that she just considers it part of your home's decor.

When Fluffy no longer thinks twice about walking past the carrier or poking her curious little nose into it, spend a few seconds here and there putting her into it. If she resists, don't try to restrain her. If she wants to leave the carrier right away, let her. Use a lot of praise before, during, and right after the carrier experience. Let Fluffy think that whenever the carrier's near she'll receive so much positive attention that all this carrier stuff is the best thing that's ever happened to her.

Don't rush. You have nothing to lose by going slowly—and everything to lose by going too quickly. When everything seems okay, repeat the procedure, but this time close the door for a second or two. Open it quickly and let Fluffy exit. Make it a game of hide-and-seek or peekaboo, complete with your most excited play-voice. Continue playing the hide-and-seek and peekaboo games in the days to come.

Once you've gotten this far, the rest is easy. Gradually increase the amount of time Fluffy spends in the carrier. Take it nice and slow, in increments of a few minutes at a time. Always have the carrier filled with Fluffy's favorite food and toys, and make a big fuss over her. If Fluffy associates great things with the carrier, you'll be well on your way to happy traveling.

DESENSITIZE FIDO TO THE CAR

Regardless of whether Fido's a novice car rider, is terrorized of the car, or tolerates the car without really enjoying it, the steps to desensitizing him are the same. Whatever you do, don't just stick Fido in the car, start the engine, and go off on your merry way unless you want to risk trauma and a carsick canine. Whenever you're dealing with—or trying to avoid—a canine psychological problem, it's best to break down the problem into the smallest possible parts and then deal with each part one at a time.

TINY LITTLE CANINE CAR STEPS

First, to minimize risk, put Fido in the parked car with you, using whatever restraining device you've chosen. (Of course, you've acclimated him to the device beforehand.) Leave the car doors open. It's important that Fido adjusts to the car without feeling restricted by being in a closed vehicle. After a few seconds, take him back in the house. Before, during, and right after this process, use lots and lots of praising, hugging, and kissing.

Once Fido thinks his quick in-and-out of the car is no big deal (this may take several days or several weeks, depending on the degree of Fido's phobia), do the same thing but with the doors closed. After a minute or two, open the doors, bring him back into the house, and, as always, use plenty of praise and love. Again, this step may take days or weeks before Fido becomes acclimated.

Next, put Fido in the car with you, close the doors, and start the engine. Let it run for a minute or so, shut it off, and take him back in the house, again using plenty of exaggerated enthusiasm. If you notice that the sound of the engine in Fido's sensitive ears sets him back dramatically, tape-record the sound and play it in the house at progressively louder volumes until he adjusts to the noise. Do the same for traffic noise if Fido finds it upsetting. Be prepared to play the recordings for a week or two, and longer if necessary.

Now that you've accomplished all this, you're ready to go for a ride. It's time to ride up and down the driveway or half a block or so. After this, turn around and drive right back home. Take this step gradually. The motion of a moving vehicle could be more than Fido's ready for. As he adjusts, increase the length of a ride to one complete block, then to around the neighborhood. If Fido has a favorite friend—canine or human—living close by, take him to the friend. Stopping the car for fun things will help break up the trip, and he'll learn to associate the car with positive activities. Take Fido to an area you think he'll enjoy—a park or the woods, for instance. As you progress you could even think about taking him on a picnic. Whatever you choose, the idea remains the same: Let Fido think that being in the car means fun and exciting things are going to happen.

WON'T THIS TAKE A LONG TIME?

This all may sound like a lot of work, but it really doesn't take more than a few minutes each day. When you stop to think of all the problems good car-travel training solves, it's well worth the effort. I know I don't have to convince anyone who's already lived through the experience of traveling with a dog that hates the carrier, the car, and everything else that goes along with it. Dogs like that don't even get to the vet regularly—the stress literally jeopardizes their health and well-being. It's worth the time to ensure Fido's happy response.

The process may be slow. If your dog is grown, fear may already be instilled in him. Just don't fall into the trap of thinking you can't teach an old(er) dog new tricks. Give him more credit than that. Okay, so your neighbors might give you funny looks as you sit in the car in your driveway with your dog—going absolutely nowhere. Who cares what they think!

NEVER, NEVER, NEVER . . .

Never allow Fluffy to hang her head out of the window of a moving car. Fluffy may love it, but road debris can lodge in her ears, eyes, and nose. One quick leap can also turn into an escape with a fatal ending.

Never leave a leash or rope in the carrier. It could strangle Fluffy.

Never leave Fluffy unattended in a car. Pet thievery and auto theft are on the rise. Also, in warm temperatures, deadly conditions can occur within minutes.

Cars parked in the shade are not exempt. As the sun moves, the shaded area changes. Be extra careful of dogs with "pushed-in" faces (such as pugs and bulldogs). Due to their facial construction, they are even more susceptible than other dogs to hot temperatures in the car. And in cold weather cars turn into freezers—in no time.

C'MON FIDO, LET'S HIT THE ROAD

Once Fido's adjusted to the car, he can see the vet regularly. He can go see Grandma or his sisters and brothers. He can go on a picnic or to a party. And he can go on vacation.

CHOOSING A BOARDING FACILITY

TIPS FOR STAYING OUT OF TROUBLE

If you've decided that Fluffy must stay behind when you go away, there are things you must know.

Years ago I owned and operated a boarding facility for pets. I know firsthand what can happen in even the best-run facilities. You see, taking care of pets is like taking care of lots of little kids; no matter how careful you try to be, things happen. In order to limit the risk of problems occurring, follow the steps I've put together for you.

Make personal inspections of facilities and stop by unannounced.

Visit a number of facilities and get educated. By making comparisons you'll be better prepared to make a decision.

Insist on seeing where the pets are kept, not just the reception room.

Arrive as early in the morning as you are allowed. This will give you an idea of the type of care the pets receive overnight. You'll also see how quick the staff is to feed and clean up after them in the morning.

Will Fluffy's cage be adequate enough for her to move around in and feel comfortable?

Although it's important to meet and evaluate the receptionist and the owner and manager of the facility, it's perhaps even more important to meet the workers in the kennel area. After all, these are the people who will be in daily contact with Fluffy, and the quality of her care will depend on them.

Check for cleanliness, not only in the middle of the floor but in the corners, too. Animal boarding facilities are perfect places for viral and bacterial threats to develop. Personnel should always be on the lookout for dirt and hair buildup.

Will the facility provide the diet Fluffy eats at home? If the answer is yes, take a look at the area where meals are prepared to verify that there is a variety of foods on hand. If the kennel will not provide the food, will you be allowed to supply it?

Does the boarding facility ask for written proof of vaccinations, or at least insist on speaking to Fluffy's vet to verify her shots? It's a problem if they are willing to take your word for it. You may be telling the truth, but other owners may not or may not realize that their pets' vaccinations are not up-to-date.

Is there a vet on call in case of emergency? If so, who? Is the vet someone you trust? Will they call your vet?

Did the receptionist ask you to fill out a questionnaire asking for pertinent information such as a phone number where you could be reached, the name and number of a close friend or relative in case of emergency, a favorite food to perk up Fluffy's appetite in case she's stressed and isn't eating, allergies to food, medication, or insect bites, etc.?

Will the facility accept Fluffy's mat or bed from home? They should. Don't wash it before the boarding stay—it should carry the family's scent so Fluffy doesn't feel so abandoned.

How much exercise will Fluffy get? How often and for how long? Check out the area where she will be walked and exercised. Is it clean? Is it well fenced in to prevent her from running away? Is there a shaded area to protect Fluffy from the heat of the midday sun if her stay takes place during the summer?

How much extra fencing is around the premises? What about

double sets of doors? If Fluffy were to get loose, would she have an easy time getting out of the building, or is it designed to contain an escapee? Sooner or later every boarding facility experiences a pet getting out of its cage. The question is: If the pet is loose, can it get off the premises?

Tip the workers before you leave on your trip. Be generous. It may ensure some extra TLC for Fluffy. Tip again when you return.

If you're going away for more than a week, be sure to have someone who knows Fluffy stop in to the facility to see her. This trusted someone should check for any obvious weight problems or illness.

As an extra safeguard, call from wherever you are and speak to the owner or manager. Even if it's a five-dollar phone call, isn't Fluffy worth the expense?

Don't be fooled into thinking that if you've found someone who will board your four-footed best friend in their own home everything will be hunky-dory. Take all the steps I've described for the larger facility. Remember, this person has opened up his or her home for business, so don't be shy about requesting an inspection of the entire place. That means back rooms, basements, and attics. Often a pet is locked away the moment the owner's out the door.

If you and Fluffy are lucky enough to have someone come into your home to take care of her, be just as careful as you would be with any other boarding decision. Fluffy's nanny should stop by a minimum of three times a day for Fluffy's walks and to check on Fluffy's food and water supply. At least one of these daily visits should be on the long side so Fluffy can have some extra playtime and special attention. Be sure the nanny knows about Fluffy's habit of trying to run out the door. I can't begin to tell you how many friends or relatives have never forgiven themselves when the pet in their charge escaped out the door, gone forever.

A TEARFUL GOOD-BYE

Of course you'll worry if Fluffy's left behind, but sometimes we just don't have any choice in these matters. Try not to feel too guilty. If you take the time and do all your boarding homework, your four-footed best friend should be just fine.

FIDO'S HEALTH
INSURANCE PLAN

DOGGY DENTISTRY

When I first started talking about doggy dentistry in the early 1970s, I was the laughingstock of the pet world. When I went on live television extolling the benefits of brushing our pets' teeth, the pet industry still hadn't caught up to me.

I am happy to say that things finally are beginning to change—and not a second too soon! Some statistics now show that the majority of all pets have some form of tooth or gum disease by the time they reach five years of age. That's a horrendous statistic!

From a purely aesthetic standpoint, how many of us have been licked on the face by an adorable, enthusiastic dog only to discover the true meaning of the term "dog breath"? Chances are that, even if the dog has been given a good bill of health by the vet, he is suffering from some type of tooth or gum disease.

What can you do to save Fluffy's teeth from suffering this dental destiny? The same thing people do to preserve their own teeth—brush them.

BRUSHING FLUFFY'S TEETH AT HOME

Breaking up plaque is the key to keeping Fluffy's mouth healthy. Brushing with a child's toothbrush or rubbing the teeth and gums with a washcloth or some gauze will do just fine. Any moderately abrasive action will help dislodge plaque.

WILL FLUFFY REMEMBER TO PUT THE CAP BACK ON THE TOOTHPASTE?

Be careful when choosing a toothpaste. Don't use human toothpaste on dogs—it can have negative effects, such as upsetting their stomachs. Instead, speak to your vet about using baking soda or a baking soda/hydrogen peroxide combination. Yes, there are even several toothpastes made especially for dogs available on the market!

WILL FLUFFY TOLERATE YOUR DENTAL DOINGS?

Don't expect the average canine to greet you with open paws when it comes to brushing her teeth. I don't know too many young kids that are thrilled by brushing their teeth, either. However, as time goes on, most of those kids get used to the idea and find brushing more agreeable. Fluffy will never get to the point of being able to brush and floss her own teeth, but she will start to let you brush them for her.

Don't even consider any mouth-cleaning attempts unless Fluffy is thoroughly accustomed to being handled. If she's the type that won't even tolerate being held on your lap, you're certainly not ready for doggy dentistry. But if she's come to trust you handling her or if you've gained better control over her from applying some of the educational techniques in this book, you're ready to roll.

TIPS TO HELP THE NO-WAY-AM-I-GOING-TO-SIT-STILL-FOR-THIS DOGGY

Forget about brushing for a while and just get Fluffy used to having your hands around her mouth. Use a few treats or a little doggy massage so that she comes to understand that your hands being around her mouth doesn't pose a threat.

Leave a toothbrush, washcloth, or a small piece of gauze around her toys or sleeping area for a week or two. Let her come to see it in a nonthreatening way.

If Fluffy still acts like she'd rather die than have her teeth brushed, try putting some chicken soup, a little beef bouillon, or even some specially flavored dog food on the brushing apparatus. In other words, place one of Fluffy's favorite foods on the toothbrush, cloth, or gauze. Most dogs are a lot more receptive when they associate the brushing apparatus with something that is great-tasting.

If necessary, start with a slow and gentle pass at the mouth and lips, and don't even think about going inside the mouth until Fluffy seems relaxed about the whole affair.

When you're ready to brush the teeth, do it only for a second or two. Stop and praise Fluffy elaborately. After every five or ten attempts, increase the amount of time spent brushing by a few more seconds.

WILL SHE GARGLE?

No, but she may bite. This is not meant to scare you—it simply means that if you haven't followed the necessary prerequisite steps for socializing and handling Fluffy, don't expect things to fall right into place. Only owners who have developed a mutual trust with their dog will be successful at good oral hygiene for Fluffy.

DOES FIDO HAVE TO BRUSH
AFTER EVERY MEAL?

Fido doesn't need to have his teeth done two, three, or four times a day. However, once a day would be ideal. If you can't manage that, at least try to work it in every other day.

DOES FIDO HAVE TO BRUSH IF HE EATS
HARD BISCUITS REGULARLY?

Remember how you were told when you were growing up that apples, celery, carrots, and other firm fruits and vegetables were nature's toothbrushes? Your parents probably encouraged you to eat them, but they still insisted that you brush your teeth. In other words, eating firm fruits and vegetables were an adjunct to brushing, not a replacement for it. The same goes for dog biscuits.

BRUSHING ALONE IS NOT ENOUGH

Fido still needs dental care provided by the vet. Professional cleanings are important. Without it, Fido may end up like the vast majority of dogs, who suffer tooth loss and gum disease.

WHAT'S THE BIG DEAL IF FIDO HAS SOME
DENTAL PROBLEMS AS HE GETS OLDER?

It's a very big deal if Fido's oral needs aren't met. Infection of the mouth can spread throughout the body and create one very sick dog. Also, mouth discomfort may prevent Fido from eating properly—or at all. If Fido drools, stands over his food dish looking like he's interested but won't eat, or goes up to the dish, walks away, returns and continues to repeat the process, his dental problems may already be quite serious. Brushing Fido's teeth may sound silly, but it's quite the opposite. It is a very important part of his health insurance plan.

YOU COULD BE KILLING YOUR DOG

Take a few minutes and crawl around the floor. See the world from Fluffy's perspective. Keep an eye out for what could harm her. If you do, I bet you'll notice a few things you never considered before. Extension cords dangling from outlets look inviting to puppies who like to chew. Those dieffenbachia plants, right within Fluffy's reach, could be deadly if eaten. There are dozens of ways even the most caring dog owners can harm their pets. Let common sense be your guide. Take a good hard look at anything that's a part of Fluffy's life and ask yourself what's wrong. If you can't find something hazardous to Fluffy, you're probably not looking hard enough.

IN YOUR HOME

We all know that dogs can't fly (except on planes). Why, then, do we often hear stories of dogs ending up splattered on the ground? While more frequently associated with cats, dogs also can be victims of the so-called high-rise syndrome. Keep screens or protective bars narrow enough that Fluffy can't squeeze through on all open windows.

If your home features a fireplace or wood-burning stove, be sure there's enough protective screening surrounding it so Fluffy doesn't singe her paws and fur.

Don't leave sharp items lying on your countertops. If Fluffy were to get up on her hind legs to investigate (provided that Fluffy's not a dachshund), she could slice her paws. Of course be careful with knives, but don't forget about razors and scissors.

Where do you store household cleaners and poisons? I bet

there are a lot of these products tucked away under the kitchen and bathroom sinks, or on shelves Fluffy can reach. It doesn't take much to kill a dog. Keep your dangerous household products out of Fluffy's reach, or at least install childproof locks on your undersink cabinets. I won't relay the gruesome details of what happened to one pet who taste-tested a chemical drain opener. It goes without saying what the substance did to the mouth, throat, and stomach of this poor animal.

There's usually at least one member of every family who's taking some form of prescription medication. Where's the bottle kept? Too often it is left on a nightstand or a kitchen table—all within Fluffy's reach.

Are there bones in the garbage? Can Fluffy raid the pail? Even a small bone, if lodged in just the right position, can kill her. For this reason, never give Fluffy a real bone to chew on. I recommend rawhide bones instead.

Did you know that your loose change could be killing Fluffy? Pennies minted after 1982 contain a high zinc content. If your dog's stomach acid eats away at the zinc, Fluffy could be poisoned.

OUTSIDE YOUR HOME

Lots of plants, flowers, and shrubs are dangerous to dogs. A little nibble is often all it takes. The list of potentially dangerous greenery is very lengthy. It's best that you check with your local garden center about them.

When spring and summertime roll around, are you guilty of spreading chemicals and fertilizers on your lawn, then allowing Fluffy and other neighborhood animals to walk on it? If Fluffy gets a little on her paws and licks it off, she could become quite ill. If she ingests enough of it, she could even die. And if you don't use such products, do you let Fluffy roam on the lawns of neighbors who do?

Tools, especially gardening tools, have sharp points that can easily puncture paws or even poke out an eye.

Great-smelling odors filter off the barbecue. If cookouts are part of your lifestyle, make sure to keep Fluffy away from the hot grill.

Antifreeze can be a serious problem. Its sweet taste actually attracts animals. I think you can guess the result by now. So be sure to check for leaks under cars in your driveway and on the street.

Speaking of cars, never leave Fluffy unattended in the car—no matter what the weather is outside. When it's warm out, our cars heat up fast and Fluffy could bake (or die) in no time. In cold temperatures automobiles can rapidly become iceboxes. And don't lull yourself into a false sense of security just because you keep the car windows open for Fluffy during the warmer weather. You don't know how many heart-broken owners have told me they left their pets unattended "for just a few minutes" and returned to find their beloved pets suffering from heat exhaustion or worse. Some well-meaning owners, leaving their car windows open, have returned to find that their pets have been stolen.

HOLIDAY ALERT

Keep Fluffy's safety in mind during the holidays. Decorations mean big trouble for our pets. Christmas trees get knocked down easily, so always place the tree out of Fluffy's reach or tie it onto something sturdy. The extra extension cords used for tree lights often get chewed, decorative candles tip over, and tinsel gets stuck in throats. Glass decorations shatter on the floor, and paws get cut. Turkey bones, which have the tendency to splinter, are in abundance. So is chocolate. You should never give your dogs chocolate, because it contains theobromine, which can be toxic to your four-footed best friends.

On Memorial Day, the Fourth of July, and Labor Day, there's often company running in and out of the house. Open doors are an open invitation to Fluffy. And remember those hot barbeque grills.

DON'T NEGLECT FLUFFY'S MEDICAL CARE

Owners who do not recognize Fluffy's need for veterinary attention greatly endanger their pet's health and welfare. Simple items such as yearly physical exams and routine vaccinations are frequently delayed or overlooked completely. Many ailments and life-threatening diseases are preventable, but only if Fluffy sees the doctor on schedule.

Also, be alert for signs of Fluffy straining when relieving herself, and for urine that contains blood.

ANTICIPATE

Be a responsible owner. Try to prevent any possible tragedy. No checklist could contain everything that might harm Fluffy. Look, look, look, and look again at everything in and around your home. Inspect your basement, garage, and tool shed. I bet there are lots of dangerous items stored there. Don't fool yourself into thinking that Fluffy is safe because she isn't allowed in those areas. It only takes one time! Be sure you're not jeopardizing the safety and even the life of your beloved pets.

FIDO'S DIET AND NUTRITION

Fido can select from dry food, canned food, semimoist food, or table food; all-natural, vegetable protein, animal protein, high-calorie, or low-calorie; and much, much more. Due to my high profile in the animal field, I am contacted on nearly a daily basis by pet-food manufacturers wanting to inform me of their latest products.

Even if you're the average pet owner, the dietary options are mind-boggling. Just take a stroll down the pet-food aisle at your local supermarket. Help! Just how is a dog owner supposed to know what's best?

It's a difficult question to answer. Fortunately for Fido, pet-food manufacturers are taking diet and nutrition more seriously than ever before. Many vets are also hopping on the bandwagon. The only problem is that pet nutrition was in the dark ages for so long that it's probably going to be a long time before we have all the necessary information. Now, I don't want this to sound like the vets and pet-food companies didn't care. I don't believe that was the case. Quite the contrary, millions of dollars have been poured into research to develop good products. It's just that the concept that good nutrition leads to good health and disease prevention wasn't as strongly emphasized—for pets and even for their owners—until relatively recently.

I suspect almost any suggestion I make regarding our pets' nutrition may be outdated by the time the next batch of studies comes in—and even those results may be quickly modified by subsequent findings. Therefore, check with your vet, read labels carefully, and use common sense.

STAY EDUCATED

Most pet-food companies have customer service representatives who will answer your questions and send you literature about their products. Keep informed. Call them frequently. Nudge them. I'm a firm believer in the old saying, "The squeaky wheel gets the oil."

Be sure your vet takes diet and nutrition seriously. If he or she brushes off your questions on nutrition, find another vet. An animal can only be as strong and healthy as what goes into his or her body. Just as in people, deficiencies are bound to cause problems. In fact, one relatively new area of animal nutrition I am particularly excited about is supplementation. Years ago, people who took vitamins and minerals were labeled health nuts. Now this form of dietary supplementation is widely accepted and even encouraged by many members of the medical community. Why shouldn't our pets enjoy the benefits of supplementation, as well? Of course, before adding anything unusual to your pet's diet, be sure to consult with your veterinarian.

Puppies, senior dogs, overweight dogs, and dogs with heart and kidney problems, among others, may benefit from dietary adjustments. Be sure to review this thoroughly with Fido's vet. Don't just tag along on the conversation—be assertive. Take charge if you have to. Be sure both you and the vet give diet and nutrition the attention they deserve.

VARIETY IS THE SPICE OF LIFE

Variety may be the best insurance that Fido's eating a healthy, balanced diet. Dogs who eat only one type of food day in and day out, all year long, become totally dependent on that food being balanced and nutritious. If Fido's tummy can tolerate it, give him different flavors three or four times a week.

WHEN I'M EATING AND FLUFFY LOOKS UP AT ME, I JUST HAVE TO GIVE IN

As a recognized pet expert I'm supposed to say, "Never give Fluffy table scraps!" But as a dog owner, of course I give Tige table scraps. He wouldn't let me live in peace unless I did. The key here is moderation. A little bit here and there added to a balanced diet won't hurt. Notice that I said "added" to a balanced diet, not replacing it. Use common sense and stay away from spicy and fatty foods. When those big eyes look up and plead "feed me," don't feel guilty about giving in. Just don't go overboard.

FAT DOGS/SKINNY DOGS

Canine obesity is one of the most common problems seen by vets. Please don't allow Fluffy to gain those extra pounds. It's not good for her. Have the vet check her, and then, if she's healthy, feed her less (but in several small meals). Increase her exercise. Be sure Fluffy's doc knows about any reducing program you have planned. The vet may have certain suggestions or certain limitations in mind.

On the other hand, if Fluffy's weight seems okay but you're worried she's not eating enough, stop worrying! Obviously, Fluffy's eating sufficiently for her metabolic rate.

As a general rule of thumb, you can get an idea if Fluffy's poundage is too much or too little by feeling her ribs. They shouldn't protrude, nor should they be buried under layers of fat.

If Fluffy's really too thin and you're worried about it, make sure she's healthy. If the vet gives her a clean bill of health, try feeding her five, six, or even seven small meals each day. I know it's a bit of extra work; however, some dogs just aren't interested in large meals. Some prefer to nosh on fresh food rather than food that's been sitting around for a few hours.

IS FIDO DRINKING?

Some dogs just don't drink enough water, and this can lead to a variety of medical problems. My dog Tige isn't a water drinker. To compensate for this, I add some water to his dry food, making it soupy so that he laps it up. Another alternative is adding just a few drops of milk to his water to make it more appealing. Finally, during the summer, when the heat increases the chances of dehydration, I treat Tige to a little bit of water-melon—seeds removed, of course. Watermelon happens to be Tige's favorite food in the world. Perhaps your four-footed best friend would enjoy it, too.

DON'T UNDERESTIMATE THE VALUE OF DIET

Keeping Fido on a proper diet is the single most important thing you can do to help ensure that he remains healthy, loving, and bright-eyed and bushy-tailed.

DOGGY MAKEOVERS

We've all watched makeovers on television, as working women and moms were transformed into glamorous females, or construction workers and executives were turned into handsome and sophisticated hunks. It's not that the basic elements for the transformations weren't there all the time. It's just that we don't always know how to best enhance our personal appearance.

Fluffy has the same problem. We're not always aware of her beauty and grooming needs. In fact, one of the most memorable television segments I've done involves taking a couple of four-footed "models" from a local shelter and transforming them into canine knockouts. In addition to boosting their looks and spirits, I am happy to say these four-footed Pygmalions are usually adopted immediately!

So if your dog is looking a little disheveled, it might be just the time for a doggy makeover. The family pet may be unrecognizable after a good shampoo and conditioning, a hair styling, blow dry, and pedicure. Clearly Fluffy will look and smell better, but a makeover may make her feel better, both physically and emotionally. That's why good candidates for a new look include adult pets that have been pushed into the background after their novelty has worn off, bored and lonely pets that are left alone all day, senior citizen pets, and pets that are depressed. Come on, you know how good it feels after taking a shower, getting a new hairstyle, or being pampered at a salon!

EASY STEPS TO ADJUST FLUFFY TO BATHTIME

Many of our dogs, especially the water-loving breeds, don't offer any resistance when it comes to bathtime. Others, such as my friend's dog Missy, hide under the bed when the terrible "B-word" (bath) is mentioned.

It's best to get Fluffy used to bathtime when she's young; however, older dogs can become adjusted to the bathing experience. Of course, don't just toss Fluffy into the water and expect her to enjoy it. Take the time to gradually adjust her to the experience.

First, decide which sink or tub you're going to use. Place a nonskid rubber mat on the bottom so Fluffy can get her footing and feel secure.

When you're ready, put a collar on Fluffy so you have something to hold on to. Place her in the sink or tub—without water. Repeat this for a few days or weeks until she seems relaxed. If necessary, place some of her favorite toys or food in with her. Don't expect her to be interested in them the first few times.

Put a little warm water (check the temperature carefully) in the bottom of the sink or tub. Not a lot—just enough to wet her toes. Practice this a few more times.

Show Fluffy the spray attachment, but don't use it yet.

Once nothing's scaring her, spray a little water out of the attachment, pointing it away from her until you're sure she's not afraid of it.

🐾 *It's Bathtime!* Bathe Fluffy early in the day so she isn't damp at bedtime. Wait for a warm day or make sure your home is nice and toasty.

Brush her well to remove all loose, dead hair. A good dog brush is essential. Brush in the direction of, as well as against, the coat. Also, brush to the skin, not just the top layer of hair. Rub a damp washcloth over the dog, again both in the direction of and against the coat. It will help remove even more loose hair.

Put a cotton ball moistened with a little mineral oil in each of Fluffy's ears. This will help prevent water from entering the ear area. If Fluffy's not thrilled about this cotton ball stuff, practice doing it outside of the sink or tub until she accepts it.

Some people advise using a drop of mineral oil around the eyes to lessen any irritation caused by shampoo or water in the eyes.

Shampoo Fluffy with a shampoo made exclusively for dogs. Take advantage of special shampoos. There are shampoos to brighten the coats of white-haired dogs, shampoos to bring out the luster of black-coated canines, conditioners and detanglers for long-coated breeds, medicated shampoos for dry coats and those with fleas. Try to select a tearless variety, if possible. Whatever type you choose, be sure to read all the directions carefully and rinse Fluffy thoroughly.

Always towel-dry Fluffy completely. If you can get her adjusted to a hair dryer, all the better. Let her get used to seeing the dryer when it's not operating, then let her adjust to it when it's blowing at a distance. Gradually decrease the distance between her and the dryer. Be sure the dryer's temperature is low to medium. Don't let it get too hot!

Brush her a little bit here and there while she's drying. And there you'll have it—one very clean and fresh-smelling doggy!

🐾 *Bathing Tricks of the Grooming Trade.* When Fluffy's between baths, try brushing a little cornstarch through her coat. It's the perfect dry shampoo.

If Fluffy's light-colored fur is stained, apply a lemon-juice-and-water spray to the stain, using extreme care around her eyes. Allow it to sit on the hair before bathing. The lemon juice may very well remove or lighten the stain.

WHEN DOES FIDO NEED A HAIRCUT?

With the exception of a few breeds that are supposed to have long, shaggy hair, it's pretty easy to determine when it's time for a dog to have a haircut. Overgrown hair creates long bangs that obscure Fido's vision. Hair hanging from the tips of his ears winds up dangling in his food bowl, collecting food and water. So does excessive hair in the mouth and chin areas.

🐾 *Creating Your Own Canine Coif.* Makeovers, in the form of haircuts, can be performed by professional dog groomers, but pet owners can do a lot themselves in their homes. It's not necessary to use an electric clipper, which requires a more experienced hand, but a good pair of scissors made for haircutting, generally available at drugstores, can help any owner turn a scraggly pooch into a real Prince Charming.

Hair hanging in front of Fido's eyes can be trimmed away. Of course, use extreme care that the point of the scissors is directed away from his eyes. Leave a one- or two-inch ridge of hair above his eyes to act as an awning, providing some protection from direct sun. Fido's ears can be freed from long hair fringes by neatly trimming around the outline of his ears, leaving a half-inch border. You can also follow the outline of Fido's mouth and chin area to trim away excess beard hair if it tends to become discolored and encrusted with food particles. While you have the scissors out, check the bottom of Fido's feet for excess hair between his pads. Hair extending beyond the pads should be trimmed, as grit and gravel will often become entangled in the hair, creating sores between the pads. Uneven hair under Fido's belly can also be cleaned up with the scissors, as can excessive hair on Fido's tail. With only scissors for equipment, almost any owner can give their four-footed best friend a new look.

FLUFFY NEEDS A MANICURE
(OR SHOULD I SAY PEDICURE?)

Fluffy's toe nails require frequent trimming. Occasional trimming by her vet or groomer is not always enough. Nail trimming should not be trivialized. After all, long nails can help create or aggravate arthritis, contribute to hip dysplasia, and alter the way Fluffy distributes her weight when she stands.

It's easy to determine when a nail trimming is due: Just listen for the telltale clicks of Fluffy's nails as she walks across a tile or wood floor.

🐾 *Doing It Yourself Isn't So Bad.* Clipping a dog's nails is probably the one thing about dog ownership that frightens people most. No need for that fear! Once Fluffy is comfortable with being touched (see section on "Doggy Massage," page 203), nail clipping is easy. There's one simple trick—just clip the very ends of the tips of the nails. Don't try to take too much off in one sitting. Clip only the tips. Wait a couple weeks and clip just the tips again. The vein that everyone's afraid of cutting will recede during that two-week waiting period. Try to locate the vein before you clip—on some nails you can actually see where it ends.

Use a nail clipper made specifically for dogs and have a blood-stopping product, alum powder, or a bar of soap on hand just in case you clip the nails too short. Products are available at the pet shop specifically for this purpose. Don't feel too bad if you make the nail bleed. Yes, it does hurt Fluffy—the way it hurts if you break your nail below the quick. It stings, sure, but you certainly survive. Everyone, including veterinarians and professional dog groomers, will occasionally cut a nail too short. If this happens to you, at least you know you're in good company.

There's one big advantage to being Fluffy's manicurist—you can keep the nails in good shape and at the right length. When Fluffy's nails are long, the vet or groomer can cut them back only so far—the quick in the nail needs time to recede. The end result is that Fluffy's nails are still too long. Unless you return repeatedly for nail clipping they'll never get trimmed to the proper, healthy length.

Do it with the vet or groomer the first time to be sure you understand the process. Just be brave!

WHY IT'S SO IMPORTANT TO GIVE
THOSE EARS A SNIFF

Infected ears frequently create an odor you can smell. Okay, so you have to stick your nose in Fido's ear, but early detection of an ear problem makes it worthwhile. Of course, see Fido's doc if you suspect anything is amiss.

For general cleaning purposes, use a little mineral oil on a cotton ball—not a Q-Tip—and swab only the outer parts of the inside of Fido's ear. Don't go too deep—you could injure his ear.

If there's excessive hair growth around the outer edges of the inside part of the ear and it's collecting all sorts of dirt and gunk, trim it back carefully. But, please: no scissors in the ear.

FLUFFY HAS FLEAS

Oh no, Fluffy has fleas and we're all scratching. Well, get the jump on fleas (and ticks) before they get a jump on you. That's the most important step. Don't wait until fleas take over your home before you go into action. And with the tick-related spread of Lyme disease, now more than ever before owners need to be concerned about these parasites as well.

Everybody has their own favorite flea and tick approach. There are flea collars, shampoos, dips, sprays, and powders. Whichever you use, be sure to read the directions carefully. If it's a chemical you're using, make sure you don't misuse the product. If you use more than the manufacturer recommends or use it on a very young or old dog, it may make your pet very ill. It may even kill your pet—so be careful!

Be sure to check Fluffy regularly for fleas. An easy way to do this is to roll her in a white towel. If fleas are present, they will appear on the towel, as will their droppings.

Many people treat their pets but forget about treating the home environment. Getting the fleas off Fluffy is futile if they are in the carpet and furniture, too. They'll find Fluffy again. And again. If you need to, call in an exterminator or pack up all living creatures and set off a flea bomb or defogger (available at pet shops and most hardware stores). You may need more than one bomb, depending on the square footage of your home. Again, read and follow the directions carefully. You'll probably need to cover counters and put away food products. Leave home for the recommended period of time—it's an ideal time to get Fluffy dipped or flea-shampooed. Remember, you're dealing with chemicals, so be a careful consumer.

Vacuum well, including the furniture, Fluffy's bedding (and yours if she sleeps with you), and all nooks and crannies. Cut up a flea collar and place it in the vacuum cleaner bag. This will ensure that the fleas and eggs you vacuum up will not survive. Otherwise, immediately throw out the bag or empty the container in the outside trash.

If your home is heavily infested and you are using the bomb method, you may have to repeat the process in a week or two, depending on the manufacturer's suggestion.

In a new flea-treatment breakthrough, some manufacturers now offer a nontoxic indoor treatment that is said to be as safe as table salt and does not require you or your pet to vacate the premises.

Finally, if your dog spends time in your yard, I would recommend calling in a professional to treat the outside, too.

🐾 *The Natural Approach.* Some specialists advocate a natural approach to flea control, including the use of natural, nontoxic flea shampoos. Some suggest adding brewers yeast to Fluffy's food each day—one tablespoon for every fifty pounds of pooch. Others recommend the addition of one to two cloves of garlic to Fluffy's food. One drop of pennyroyal oil (available at health food stores) on your pet's leather, nylon, or cloth collar is said to aid in flea prevention.

If you're thinking about a natural approach to fleas, check with your vet or a vet specializing in holistic medicine.

WHAT A GORGEOUS DOGGY!

When you're all done with Fluffy's makeover, just watch her strut her stuff. She feels better and she knows she looks better. Think I'm kidding? Give it a whirl. Find out for yourself.

THE HEIMLICH MANEUVER

If you walked into a room and found Fido choking, would you know what to do? If you're like the majority of owners, you may not have the slightest idea of what needs to be done to save your dog's life. Well, you've probably heard of the Heimlich maneuver for people who are choking—but did you know there's a similar procedure for Fido? All owners should know how to perform this simple maneuver. Be prepared to step in and, hopefully, ward off a disaster if a curious and unsuspecting Fido gets something caught in his throat or simply chokes on some food.

IF FIDO IS CHOKING

Open his mouth and see if the object can be removed from his throat. If it can, simply reach in with your finger and pull it out.

If Fido is conscious, there is no guarantee you might not be bitten. Of course, if Fido is accustomed to having you handle his mouth (see the section on doggy dentistry) this will be less likely to occur.

Personally, when my animals are in trouble I really don't care about a bite or a scratch. I just do what has to be done to save a life.

THE HEIMLICH MANEUVER:
HOW TO GIVE THE "HUG OF LIFE"

It's important to remain as calm as possible.

Place Fido on his side on a hard surface.

Place both hands just behind the last rib.

Press down with a fast and firm motion, moving your hands slightly forward as you do. Have your vet show you how hard to push down. Quickly release the pressure from your hands. Repeat several times in quick succession.

If you find it easier to get to Fido while he's standing up, straddle him, placing one of your legs on either side of him. Place your hands behind the last rib on either side of Fido, lift up quickly and firmly, moving your hands slightly forward as you do.

Repeat several times in quick succession.

Open his mouth and see if you can retrieve the object from Fido's throat. If other people are present, continue compressing the chest while someone else tries to remove the object from Fido's throat.

Contact your veterinarian immediately, even if Fido seems fine. Remember, as with humans, first aid is the immediate care given to your pet until proper medical care arrives.

Always review any first-aid procedure with Fido's veterinarian. Please do yourself, Fido, and me a favor. Put down this book and call the vet now. Set up a ten-minute appointment in order to review this life-saving procedure. It may turn out to be the best thing you ever do for your dog!

GETTING A SECOND OPINION

If there's anything serious going on with Fluffy's health, be sure to speak to more than one veterinarian. Pet owners are frequently loyal to their pet's doctor to a fault, not wanting to offend the vet by seeing someone else. Well, most vets are extremely professional and will not hold it against you if you seek out another opinion. In fact, many encourage it. If Fluffy's vet becomes annoyed because you want to get a second opinion, it's time to get a new vet. Fido is a member of the family. If any other member of the family were ill and the doctor's advice wasn't adding up, wouldn't you find another doctor? You bet you would. Do the same for your four-footed best friend. It's only fair.

WHEN TO GET A SECOND OPINION

- Any time surgery is suggested.

- Any time Fluffy is being treated for something and it isn't clearing up like the vet said it would.

- Any time you have that feeling in the pit of your stomach that things just aren't right or the vet's advice doesn't seem to make sense. Trust your instincts.

WHAT ABOUT A SPECIALIST?

Absolutely see a specialist if you're dealing with a medical specialty. In addition to limiting their practices to dogs, some veterinarians specialize in allergies, cancer, heart problems, orthopedic problems, and just about anything else.

If you're having trouble getting a recommendation for a specialist, contact the veterinary medical association in your county or state. They're often listed in the telephone directory. The reference desk at the public library may also have a listing for the association closest to you.

WHAT IF I DON'T AGREE WITH
THE SECOND OPINION?

It's not uncommon for owners to be dissatisfied with a second opinion. If you have the slightest doubt about what's being suggested, by all means get a third or even fourth opinion. I'm not suggesting you throw away your money and continue looking for a doctor until you find one who tells you what you want to hear. I am simply saying many times the owner knows best. Owners may not be trained in the medical sciences, but they do know their dogs. Sometimes their suspicions are more correct than any scientifically based diagnosis.

Let your heart and instinct be your guides.

HOLISTIC MEDICINE,
ACUPUNCTURE, AND CHIROPRACTIC

There are many great things now taking place in veterinary medicine. I strongly suggest that all pet owners stay abreast of new trends in medicine. Sometimes medical practitioners are like wheelbarrows—they're useful tools, but they need to be pushed. That's not to say veterinarians are incompetent or ineffective. It simply means that, very often, educated owners can bring out the best in a vet. Let your doctor know that you're on top of what's going on.

And what is going on is very exciting. New areas of medicine (they're not really so new—they've just been pooh-poohed up to now by a lot of health care professionals) are becoming much more widely accepted for both human and animal applications. Many pets are reaping the benefits of a different way of human thinking.

Traditional medicine is still of primary importance to me, but I firmly believe that there are times when other forms of medicine may complement the conventional treatment.

HOLISTIC MEDICINE

The word holistic is defined as whole, overall. Veterinarians who practice holistic medicine try to treat the entire pet, not just illnesses as they arise. These veterinarians believe that to most successfully treat pets, every factor in their lives must be taken into consideration—nutrition, exercise, home environment, daily stress, even the psychological makeup of the human family members. Based on what we know about the human animal's need for balancing all these factors, it's a very interesting idea. Many pet owners believe in this concept to some degree. The lack of a total veterinary approach has been a major complaint of many pet owners about the medical community, but of late there appears to have been a reversal. Now we hear the word holistic more often than ever before, and we hear it in the context of our pets.

Holistic vets often place an emphasis on vitamins, minerals, and diets free of chemicals and preservatives. In times of illness they often prescribe a vitamin/mineral complement to help the healing process or boost Fluffy's immune system. Some holistic vets even use herbs and plant recipes.

Before you disregard this as some sort of black magic, remember that many traditional human medications are derived from plants, roots, herbs, and the like.

Tige and I have had our own experience with the holistic approach. Several years ago he was put on medication for a bone disease. I consulted with a holistic vet, who informed me that this medication would surpress Tige's immune system. To compensate for this side effect, the holistic vet put Tige on a regimen of vitamins and minerals. Needless to say, the approach worked well and Tige is still with me and doing great!

ACUPUNCTURE

The Eastern art of acupuncture was frowned upon by Western medicine for centuries. But it seems its time has finally come. Acupuncture uses needles, which are pushed into certain sensory pathways under the skin to open up the pathways and heal other areas. Acupuncture is generally accepted now, although sometimes unwillingly, by the veterinary community. Some of the world's leading veterinary colleges and hospitals now use, and therefore lend credibility to, this ancient medical form.

CHIROPRACTIC

Chiropractic is now more widely accepted for people than ever before. Years ago, chiropractors were hard-pressed to remain free from being labeled as quacks. Today it's not uncommon for medical doctors to refer their patients to chiropractors. Often insurance carriers even cover the costs. Things certainly have changed in the chiropractic field. It's not surprising that pets can also enjoy many of the same benefits people derive from chiropractic. However, there are only a few veterinarians trained in chiropractic. More common are chiropractors for people who work on pets as well. In the case of a well-educated chiropractor who has thoroughly studied Fluffy's anatomy and who works under the supervision of a licensed vet, the lack of a veterinary degree may be acceptable. My fear, however, is that a chiropractor may jump into the animal field without a solid background in the anatomy of the domestic pet.

CHOOSE CAREFULLY

We're lucky there are veterinarians and other trained medical personnel specializing in holistic medicine, acupuncture, and chiropractic. Many have excellent reputations. However, as with any up-and-coming trend, watch out for specialists who veer away from common sense. Pay attention to any new trends and players in veterinary care—and watch out for the quacks.

SENIOR CITIZEN DOGS NEED SPECIAL CARE: WHAT YOU CAN DO TO EXTEND YOUR PET'S LIFE

It's easy to know when Fido is getting older. Either we notice it on the calendar or we become aware of his belly drooping closer to the floor. We see that his muzzle is turning gray or once-active Fido is sneaking off for a few extra naps in the sun.

As our four-footed best friends grow into their golden years, lots of things start to happen. Some are inevitable. Although old age brings irreversible changes to the body and, sometimes, to behavior, it's a very individual thing. While there is often a relationship between longevity and breed, each dog has his or her own biological clock. While many dogs live from ten to sixteen years, there are more than a few that live beyond sixteen. In addition to good genes, longevity depends on the lifestyle and environment provided by the owner.

Problems occur when owners don't pay attention to Fido's signs of aging. I think it's because we don't want to consciously acknowledge that our four-footed best friend is getting on in years. We sort of pretend he is immortal and that the final day will never come.

On the other hand, some owners believe there are seasons of life and that when a pet is in the fall and winter of his life, you must simply accept the things you cannot change. In my opinion, nothing could be further from the truth! There are plenty of ways Fido can be helped through his years of old age. By giving Fido special senior citizen care you might very well end up extending his life, adding both quality and quantity to his golden years.

NEXT PATIENT, PLEASE

The easiest and most important thing you can do is to arrange for senior Fido to see the veterinarian regularly. For old-timers, regularly means more than once a year. Make at least two trips a year, preferably three or four. You don't know how many people neglect these visits—visits that help nip old-age problems in the bud. Be sure you're dealing with a vet who understands the importance of preventive medicine with the geriatric dog. Don't allow any quick once-over exams and a declaration that Fido's fit until the next appointment.

Kidneys are often the first major organ to deteriorate, so be sure Fido gets a simple blood test for kidney function during each visit. Since the kidneys are the body's filtering system, any slowdown should be noted as soon as it happens. Preventive steps can be taken before a fatal shutdown.

Inquire about changing Fido's diet. Age-weakened organs don't always process food the way they should. Dietary adjustments can definitely lengthen Fido's life and keep him healthy through his golden years. Find out if your vet recommends one of the dog foods especially formulated for senior dogs.

You might also want to discuss with the vet the possibility of placing your graying canine on a vitamin supplement regime. Although I don't believe in megadoses of vitamins for any animal, I like to give seniors a regular dose of an old-fashioned multivitamin/mineral supplement. Their systems don't always work the way they used to, and their eating habits sometimes change as they grow older. I believe a good multivitamin/mineral supplement is sort of like Mom's chicken soup when you're sick—it might not help, but it certainly can't hurt. Your vet may have a different opinion, particularly if certain diseases have surfaced, so be sure to speak to the doctor about your dog's vitamin and mineral needs.

Stay alert for dental problems with your geriatric dog. Infections can be very debilitating during old age.

Be alert to Fido looking for warm places to rest. Sure, who

doesn't love to snooze in the sun or hang out near a warm radiator, but if your four-footed best friend seems to be spending more than the usual amount of time seeking warmth, speak to the vet immediately. Fido's internal thermostat may need adjusting.

NOT TOO SKINNY, NOT TOO PLUMP— BUT JUST RIGHT

Sometimes old stomachs can't tolerate as much food as they used to in one sitting. Break up senior Fido's diet into smaller meals served more frequently during the day and evening. Some old-timers prefer a little nibble and nosh here and there rather than a couple of big meals. Keep an eye out for weight loss—that could be a real warning sign of trouble ahead. Weigh your old-timer once a week. This is a simple trick if Fido is small enough to be lifted: Weigh yourself first, then weigh yourself again while holding Fido. Subtract the difference and you have his weight. Owners of larger dogs will need to rely on their powers of observation and more frequent visits to the vet. Remember that the loss of one pound or even half a pound for a small dog could be worth investigating.

Dogs with chubby tummies need to lose weight, but don't confuse them with senior dogs experiencing the sagging muscles and droopy bellies of old age. If you're unsure, just ask your vet.

Older dogs don't always drink enough water. It's extremely important to encourage water intake—Fido has to flush out his system. Add water into some of his meals; many dogs will eat their food in the soupy form created by soaking their dry food with water for an hour or so. If, on the other hand, your old pal demonstrates an increased interest in water, check with the vet right away. Increased thirst could be a symptom of a yet undiscovered problem, such as diabetes.

Stay alert to changes in hearing and eyesight. Older dogs, just like older people, often experience a decrease in the sensitivity of these senses. Vision loss sometimes reveals itself when dogs start pausing or stopping dead in their tracks when they enter a room or when there's been a change in the light. You'll notice Fido is just kind of standing there, sizing things up before moving around. Of course, if his vision has really deteriorated, you'll notice senior Fido bumping into things, particularly things not in their normal places.

Hearing loss is a little easier for owners to recognize. When Fido's unaware you're standing behind him, clap your hands or bang a metal spoon on a metal pot, beginning with the lowest possible noise level. If Fido doesn't respond, increase the volume gradually until you find the point where it's heard.

Have you noticed Fido is doing a lot more barking? Sometimes senior dogs who suffer a hearing loss bark more than they ever did before. It's not that they've just become more vocal overnight; they simply can't hear themselves the way they used to.

If loss of vision or hearing is taking its toll on your older pal, don't despair. Most dogs adjust surprisingly well to their disabilities. Give senior Fido a little time—you'll be surprised how well he'll do.

LUMPS AND BUMPS

Although cancer in canines, particularly older ones, is a serious concern, don't panic over every little lump and bump that shows up. Most of them will be harmless. However, be sure the vet sees each one. If it is cancer, there are so many medical treatments today that the outcome isn't always as grim as you may think.

OOPS—MISSED THE FIRE HYDRANT AGAIN!

If suddenly your perfectly house-trained dog is soiling unexpected places, don't be too tough on that little old puddlemaker.
There's a real possibility that Fido's losing a bit of control and
just can't wait until you're ready to take him out. As upset as you
might be, I guarantee your once thoroughly trained dog doesn't
feel too good about himself either. Embarrassment and humilia-
tion are bound to set in and take their toll on Fido's emotional
well-being before too long. He will need your nurturing attention rather than your aggravation.

Of course, take Fido to the vet in order to rule out any
possibility of infection. If your vet agrees that these "misses" are
simply the result of old age, there are several things you can do
to save Fido's self-esteem and your carpeting. The first obvious
step is to take Fido out more frequently, thus providing him
with more opportunities to relieve himself. If these accidents
occur during the night, restrict Fido's food and water consump-
tion in the early evening. Be sure to take him for his last walk
as late at night as possible. Then take him out early the next
morning. Yes, you'll have to make adjustments to your own
personal schedule, but isn't Fido and your carpeting worth it?

DOGGY DIAPERS

No, I'm not kidding! In some extreme cases, even the aforementioned steps will not be sufficient. Senior Fido has lost nearly all
control. Remember, Fido is not thrilled about this either. Instead of restricting him to a small area of the house, try a diaper-
like product specially designed for canines with this problem.
There are several such products available at pet shops or through
dog-care catalogs. The fact that these doggy diapers exist indicates that this is a fairly common problem for our four-footed
best friends in their golden years.

STAY ALERT

Watch for variations in elimination habits. A change in the number or consistency of bowel movements could be a red flag signaling a medical problem. Diarrhea is always a possible danger signal. Never let it go without talking to the vet—it can quickly debilitate any dog, particularly a senior one. At the other end of the spectrum, some of the old-timers may need the help of a stool softener for constipation. Your vet can guide you to the best selection. Also note Fido's urination habits. Be sure he is urinating freely, not too much more or less than what's been normal over the years.

EMOTIONAL AIDS TO KEEP THE OLDER DOG FEELING YOUNG

IT'S PARTY TIME

Throw a party for senior Fluffy. Nothing will perk up a senior faster than a festive occasion held in her honor.

SENIOR FIDO PLAYLAND

Don't forget about bringing home new toys and playthings for your special golden-age pal. Sure, I know you're thinking that he hasn't played with anything in years, but I bet you haven't brought much of anything home in years, either. Maybe you tried a few things here and there and, at best, there might have been an occasional playful outburst. The key is to keep the playthings rolling in—in the hope that one of the toys might be just the right one to spark some interest. At the very least, Fido will like having them around even if they are of no real use.

Think of it as the "junk" Grandma collects from the grandkids. There's no way she's going to use those shell ashtrays or plastic-woven key chains, but she sure loves to get and look at them. They're an expression of love. It's nice to know you've been remembered.

AN OLD-TIMER'S MASSAGE

Old bones and muscles might love a little doggy massage. (See section on massage, page 203.) We all get a little stiff, and sometimes arthritic, as the years go by. A gentle rubdown can be one of the nicest gifts you can give senior Fido.

SENIOR DOGGIES NEED MAKEOVERS, TOO!

Depression and that old-age lethargy can easily take hold of senior Fluffy's psyche. Combat this by keeping up with Fluffy's grooming. There's nothing worse than feeling unkempt. Believe me, a dog who used to be well groomed knows the difference when she's not.

While you're doing the extra brushing, check the length of Fluffy's toenails. Owners sometimes get a little sloppy about toenail length with older dogs. Long nails can aggravate old bones and arthritis by forcing Fluffy to stand improperly and thus incorrectly displace body weight.

FACE-TO-FACE LOVING

Sometimes we take Fluffy for granted. Golden-age Fluffy's been around for so long, she's become part of the furniture. So be sure you spend plenty of time with her on the floor, at eye level. Set aside some special time just for this purpose. If Fluffy's been allowed on the furniture all these years, you might notice that at her older age she's not making the jump up as often as she used to. She may really be missing that extra contact with you that she once enjoyed so much.

One of my New York radio program listeners encountered this problem. His dog could no longer make the jump up onto the bed to sleep with his master. The solution—my listener built a little ramp leading up the side of the bed. Now they again share the same bed. We make changes in our homes to accommodate elderly human family members, why not do the same for our four-footed ones?

THINKING ABOUT A NEW PUPPY PAL

Sometimes the best thing you can do for a golden-age dog is to bring a new bouncy furball into the house. The increased activity a puppy brings into a home may be the best prescription for adding life to your old-timer. If the two get along famously, that's great! Even if they don't, because the little one constantly annoys senior Fluffy, that's good, too, believe it or not. Even if old Fluffy is forced to spend most of her time ducking the nippy puppy, that's probably a whole lot more activity than she had before. Odds are, sooner or later, they will become best friends.

I know you're concerned you'll be putting your beloved dog's nose out of joint by bringing in competition. That may be true. But the initial tension will more than likely work itself out. The benefits of a more active lifestyle generally far outweigh the disadvantages.

BE A TRUE-BLUE FRIEND

Make sure you're very good to senior Fido. He may be a little crochety. Maybe he's a bit stiff and feeble. But Fido's been good to you for a long, long time. He's made you smile, and comforted you when you cried. Don't get sloppy about your best friend's care when he needs you most. You'll never forgive yourself if you do. Your loving pal deserves the best, particularly while the sun is setting on his time on earth.

THE FINAL
GOOD-BYE

WHEN IT'S TIME
TO SAY GOOD-BYE

One of the most difficult moments for anyone who's ever been owned by a dog is saying the final good-bye to your four-footed best friend. I don't think it ever gets any easier, no matter how many dogs you've had or how many times you have to go through it.

Knowing when to put sweet Fluffy to sleep is an incredibly hard decision to make. Sometimes the choice is mercifully made for us—Fluffy simply falls asleep one night and doesn't wake up in the morning. When death comes to a resting dog, we can at least take consolation in knowing that it was painless and that Fluffy died with dignity.

If Fluffy's been battling illness or the ravages of old age, it's very hard to know when it's the right time to take that final trip to the veterinarian. Here again, the key word is dignity. I always let that be my guiding light. I want all my pets to spend their remaining days on earth with their dignity intact, enjoying some quality of life. Once I know that's no longer possible, it's easier to come to terms with doing what must be done. It's what I'd want for myself. It's the least I can do for them.

Make your own decision when you think the time has come. Don't let others convince you. You'll know when the time is right. Base your decision on only one thing—what's right for her. Don't extend her time because you just can't bear to see her go. She lived life as a smart and clever little creature. She doesn't want her final days to be any less than that.

Please don't feel foolish if you grieve. You may even need to take off a few days from work. Not everyone will understand your sense of loss over a dog—especially people who have never been owned by one. Their feelings are of no consequence; it's a pity they've never experienced the special type of loving relationship you had with your precious pet. Grieving is a normal, healthy reaction to the loss of a beloved family member. And wasn't Fluffy a member of the family? Realize that you're not alone with those feelings. Millions of people have grieved over the loss of their four-footed pals.

If you find the pain is too great to bear yourself, contact your local humane society. Almost every area has a support group to help owners through these difficult times. You'll be able to talk about your feelings and share your stories. You'll remember the times Fluffy made you laugh. You'll remember all those funny little antics of hers. You'll remember all the love she gave you, asking nothing in return for herself. And, yes, you'll even manage a smile or two.

So, "Good-bye, dear Fluffy. No matter how much time passes, I'll never forget you. You'll be in my heart, always and forever. I love you."

&

THE NEXT
HELLO

PAWS THROUGH THE
SHELTER BARS

Just when you think your heart is broken forever and you could
never go through the pain of losing another dog, something
strange happens. You stop into the local animal shelter—perhaps
to donate some cans of dog food you found in your pantry—and
some little ball of fur reaches his paw through the bars of his cage
in an effort to get your attention. So tiny and alone, he can't be
more than seven weeks old. You know he's desperate for a
home.

Don't feel guilty. You won't be replacing Fluffy or trying
to forget about her. It's just time to go on. Think of it as
Fluffy's legacy—she left this world so another little puppy
could enjoy the special love and companionship you can provide.

So brush up on your doggy dialogue and stock up on toys
and wee-wee pads. Here comes that little ball of fur and energy. Like a flash, he races through your living room. There
he goes again, only now he's chewing on your slipper. He

drops the slipper and goes after one of your socks. You'd better keep this book around—I think you're going to need it again.

Good luck with the new one! Somehow I know you'll both do just fine.

INDEX

A

About-turn method, 138–142
Abuse, 5, 6, 120, 194–195
Active submission, 24
Acupuncture, 259
Aggression, 75, 133
  body language, 22–23
  causes of, 193–195
  eyes, 23, 32–33
  solving problem of,
    196–197
  tail, 35–36, 196
  warning signals of,
    195–196
Airline travel, 209, 215–218,
  227, 228
Alum powder, 176, 186, 251
American Kennel Club, 89
Ammonia-based products,
  105
Anal glands, 148
Answering machine messages,
  63–64

smiling, 46
submissive, 23
Litter box, 108, 213
Little-tug-and-release technique,
125–126
Longe line, 168
Longevity, 260
Lumps and bumps, 263
Lyme disease, 252

M

Makeovers, 59, 247–254, 266
Manners, 59, 186–187
Massage, 59, 203–206, 266
Mental health, 48–79
depression, 52–60
emotional tears, 67–68
introduction of second pet,
69–79
latchkey dogs, 49, 60–65,
70
mental stimulation, 50–52
midlife crisis, 65–67
recognizing emotions,
48–49
stress, 49–50
Mental stimulation, 50–52
Midlife crisis, 65–67
Minerals, 173, 244, 258, 261
Motels, 210
Mounting, 90–91

Mourning, 53
Mouthing, 177–179
Multipet families, 70

N

Nail trimming, 250–251,
266
Nature's Miracle, 106
Negative attention syndrome,
63, 174, 178, 180, 186
Neglect, 55–56
Neutering, 86–88, 91, 92
Neutral turf, 72–73, 76
New babies, introduction of,
80–84
Newspaper, 96–97
Noise, fear of, 187–190
Nonverbal communication,
21–24
Nymphomania, 91

O

Obedience training (*see*
Training)
Obesity, 199–200, 246
Observation, 39–40
Odor neutralizers, 105–106,
111

ABOUT THE AUTHOR

WARREN ECKSTEIN is a noted pet psychologist and has worked with the animals of such celebrities as David Letterman, Cheryl Tiegs, and Lily Tomlin. He has his own nationally syndicated radio show telling owners how to best treat their pets. Warren and his coauthor and wife, Andrea Eckstein, live on Long Island, New York, with their dogs, cats, pigs, and birds.